AWS Certified Solutions Architect Associate SAA-C01

AWS Certified Solutions Architect Associate Practice Test Questions
with Complete explanations and References

Set 3 of 6

Tutorials Avenue

ABOUT THIS BOOK

AWS Certified Solutions Architect Associate Practice Test Questions in with Complete explanations & References.

These AWS Certified Solutions Architect Associate practice tests are patterned after the latest exam format and updated regularly based on the feedback of our 30,000+ students on what appeared in the actual exam. Our AWS Certified Solutions Architect practice tests are TOP-NOTCH and the CLOSEST to the actual exam, as demonstrated by the 6,000++ reviews on our course.

The AWS Certified Solutions Architect Associate (SAA-C01) is consistently among the top paying IT certifications, considering that Amazon Web Services (AWS) is the leading cloud services platform in the world with almost 50% market share! Earn over $150,000 per year with an AWS Solutions Architect certification!

But before you become an AWS Certified Solutions Architect Professional, it is recommended for you to pass the AWS Solutions Architect Associate certification exam first, and this is where AWS practice tests come in. It is possible that you have read all of the available AWS documentations online yet still fail the exam! These AWS practice tests simulate the actual certification exam and ensure that you indeed understand the subject matter.

This AWS Certified Solutions Architect Associate Practice Exam course is for anyone who is looking for a study material that provides the following:

390 TOP-NOTCH Questions - has 6 sets of AWS Practice Tests with 65 UNIQUE Questions and a 130-minute time limit for each set.

SIMULATES ACTUAL EXAM ENVIRONMENT - mimics the actual, and the latest AWS Solutions Architect Associate certification exam to help you pass and even ace the AWS exam!

DETAILED explanations, REFERENCE LINKS, AND CHEAT SHEETS - our answer keys at the end of each set have full and detailed explanations along with complete reference links so you can check and verify yourself that the answers are correct. Plus, bonus cheat sheets to help you better understand the concepts.

UPDATED 2 to 3 TIMES A MONTH - we have a dedicated team updating our Question bank on a regular basis, based on the feedback of thousands of our students on what appeared on the actual exam.

MOBILE-COMPATIBLE - so you can conveniently review everywhere, anytime with your smartphone!

HAS BETTER VALUE THAN THE OFFICIAL AWS PRACTICE TEST - which is worth about $20 but only contains about 20 - 40 Questions.

CLEAR AND ERROR-FREE QUESTIONS - Each item has a reference link that can validate the answer.

Prepared by an AWS Certified Solutions Architect Professional who has actually passed the exam!

These AWS Solutions Architect practice exams are designed to focus on the important exam topics (such as EC2, EBS, S3 and many others) hence, the aforementioned topics have more Questions than the other AWS knowledge areas. The number of Questions on each topic are carefully selected based on the 5 domains of the actual AWS certification exam. Out of the 5 domains, Domain 1: Design Resilient Architectures has the highest percentage (34%) with topics such as reliable and/or resilient storage; how to design decoupling mechanisms; determine how to design multi-tier, fault tolerant architectures, etc. Note that although there is a focus on these AWS topics, the Questions are all still unique, to ensure that you fully grasp the concepts.

Some people are using brain dumps for the AWS Certified Solutions Architect certification exam which is totally absurd and highly unprofessional because these dumps will not only hinder you to attain an in-depth AWS knowledge, these can also result with you failing the actual AWS certification exam since Amazon regularly updates the exam coverage.

Please also note that these AWS Certified Solutions Architect practice tests are not brain dumps and since Amazon shuffles the actual exam content from a Question bank with hundreds to thousands of Questions, it is nearly impossible to match what you can see here with the actual tests. Again, the key to passing the exam is a good understanding of AWS services and this is what our AWS Certified Solutions Architect Associate practice tests are meant to do.

There are a lot of existing AWS Practice Tests in the market however, most of them contain both technical and grammatical errors that may cause you to fail the actual exam. There are also official certification practice exams provided by AWS but these only have 20 or 40 Questions and cost 20 or 30 USD -- a price that is comparable with having these 390 Unique and Timed Amazon Web Services practice Questions!

When I was reviewing for my AWS Certified Solutions Architect Associate exam, I had a hard time finding comprehensive practice tests to help me pass my exam. I bought some of them in the market but I was disappointed because there are a lot of technical and grammatical errors in the Questions. This is why I created these AWS practice tests to help my fellow IT professionals in the industry.

We gave a considerable amount of effort to create and publish these AWS practice tests, including the laborious task of checking each item for any errors. We are confident that this will significantly help you pass your CSA-Associate exam. And we don't need to trash or slander other AWS practice test courses here on Udemy just to make a sale because we are confident that our AWS practice tests are simply the BEST. All the best!

IMPORTANT NOTE

Remember that using this product alone does not guarantee you will pass the AWS exam as you still need to do your own readings and hands-on exercises in AWS. Nonetheless, these Amazon Web Services practice exams provide a comprehensive assessment on which knowledge area you need improvement on and even help you achieve a higher score!

WHAT YOU'LL LEARN

Increase your chances of passing the AWS Certified Solutions Architect Associate Exam

Get access to our Q&A section which has tons of information and feedback about the actual AWS exam

Answer and solve tricky scenario-based AWS Solutions Architect Questions under time pressure

Take the practice exams again and again, unlike the AWS-provided practice exam which you can only do once

Validate your answers and do further readings with the provided reference links from the Official AWS documentation

Learn the AWS concepts in-depth with the comprehensive explanations included in each answer plus bonus cheat sheets!

Learn how to design highly available and fault tolerant computer networks

Gain a better understanding of AWS technologies such as EC2, S3, VPC, RDS, Lambda, SWF and many more!

Become an AWS Certified Solutions Architect Associate!

WHO THIS COURSE IS FOR

For those who are about to take the AWS Certified Solutions Architect Associate exam

For all IT Professionals who want to gauge their AWS Knowledge for their upcoming job interview

For anyone who want to take their career, and salary, to a whole new level with an AWS certification!

TABLE OF CONTENTS

AWS CERTIFIED SOLUTIONS ARCHITECT ASSOCIATE PRACTICE TEST 3

QUESTION 1:

A VPC has a non-default public subnet which has four On-Demand EC2 instances that can be accessed over the Internet. Using the AWS CLI, you launched a fifth instance that uses the same subnet, Amazon Machine Image (AMI), and security group which are being used by the other instances. Upon testing, you are not able to access the new instance.

Which of the following is the most suitable solution to solve this problem?

A. Include the fifth EC2 instance to the Placement Group of the other four EC2 instances and enable Enhanced Networking.

B. Set up a NAT gateway to allow access to the fifth EC2 instance.

C. Configure the routing table for the public subnet to explicitly include the fifth EC2 instance.

D. Associate an Elastic IP address to the fifth EC2 instance. **(Correct)**

EXPLANATION

By default, a "default subnet" of your VPC is actually a public subnet, because the main route table sends the subnet's traffic that is destined for the internet to the internet gateway. You can make a default subnet into a private subnet by removing the route from the destination 0.0.0.0/0 to the internet gateway. However, if you do this, any EC2 instance running in that subnet can't access the internet.

Instances that you launch into a default subnet receive both a public IPv4 address and a private IPv4 address, and both public and private DNS hostnames. Instances that you launch into a nondefault subnet in a default VPC don't receive a public IPv4 address or a DNS hostname. You can change your subnet's default public IP addressing behavior

By default, nondefault subnets have the IPv4 public addressing attribute set to false, and default subnets have this attribute set to true. An exception is a nondefault subnet created by the Amazon EC2 launch instance wizard — the wizard sets the attribute to true.

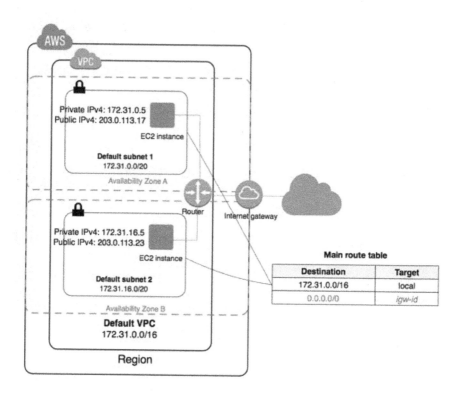

Option D is correct because the fifth instance does not have a public IP address since it was deployed on a nondefault subnet. The other 4 instances are accessible over the Internet because they each have an Elastic IP address attached, unlike the last instance which only has a private IP address. An Elastic IP address is a public IPv4 address, which is reachable from the Internet. If your instance does not have a public IPv4 address, you can associate an Elastic IP address with your instance to enable communication with the Internet.

Option A is incorrect because Placement Groups is primarily used to determine how your instances are placed on the underlying hardware while Enhanced Networking, on the other hand, is for providing high-performance networking capabilities using single root I/O virtualization (SR-IOV) on supported EC2 instance types.

Option B is incorrect because you do not need a NAT Gateway nor a NAT instance in this scenario considering that the instances are already in public subnet. Remember that a NAT Gateway or a NAT instance is primarily used to enable instances in a private subnet to connect to the Internet or other AWS services, but prevent the Internet from initiating a connection with those instances.

Option C is incorrect because all four EC2 instances which are in the same subnet, same AMI, and same security group can be accessed over the Internet. This means that there is no problem on its routing table.

Reference:
https://docs.aws.amazon.com/vpc/latest/userguide/default-vpc.html

QUESTION 2:

Your manager has asked you to deploy a mobile application that can collect votes for a popular singing competition. Millions of users from around the world will submit votes using their mobile phones. These votes must be collected and stored in a highly scalable and highly available data store which will be queried for real-time ranking.

Which of the following combination of services should you use to meet this requirement?

A. Amazon DynamoDB and AWS AppSync **(Correct)**

B. Amazon Redshift and AWS Mobile Hub

C. Amazon Relational Database Service (RDS) and Amazon MQ

D. Amazon Aurora and Amazon Cognito

EXPLANATION

When the word durability pops out, the first service that should come to your mind is Amazon S3. Since this service is not available in the answer options, we can look at the other data store available which is Amazon DynamoDB.

DynamoDB is durable, scalable, and highly available data store which can be used for real-time tabulation. You can also use AppSync with DynamoDB to make it easy for you to build collaborative apps that keep shared data updated in real time. You just specify the data for your app with simple code statements and AWS AppSync manages everything needed to keep the app data updated in real time. This will allow your app to access data in Amazon DynamoDB, trigger AWS Lambda functions, or run Amazon Elasticsearch queries and combine data from these services to provide the exact data you need for your app.

Option B is incorrect as Amazon Redshift is mainly used as a data warehouse and for online analytic processing (OLAP). Although this service can be used for this scenario, DynamoDB is still the top choice given its better durability and scalability.

Options C and D are possible answers in this scenario, however, DynamoDB is much more suitable for simple mobile apps which do not have complicated data relationships compared with enterprise web applications. The scenario says that the mobile app will be used from around the world, which is why you need a data storage service which can be supported globally. It would be a management overhead to implement multi-region deployment for your RDS and Aurora database instances compared to using the Global table feature of DynamoDB.

References:
https://aws.amazon.com/dynamodb/faqs/

https://aws.amazon.com/appsync/

Here is a deep dive on Amazon DynamoDB Design Patterns:

https://youtu.be/HaEPXoXVf2k

QUESTION 3:

You were recently promoted to a technical lead role in your DevOps team. Your company has an existing VPC which is quite un-

utilized for the past few months. The business manager instructed you to integrate your on-premises data center and your VPC. You explained the list of tasks that you'll be doing and mentioned about a Virtual Private Network (VPN) connection. The business manager is not tech-savvy but he is interested to know what a VPN is and its benefits.

What is one of the major advantages of having a VPN in AWS?

A. Security is automatically managed by AWS.

B. You can connect your AWS cloud resources to on-premises data centers using VPN connections. **(Correct)**

C. You can provision unlimited number of Amazon S3 and Glacier resources.

D. None of the above

EXPLANATION

Option B is correct. One main advantage of having a VPN connection is that you will be able to connect your Amazon VPC to other remote networks.

You can create an IPsec VPN connection between your VPC and your remote network. On the AWS side of the VPN connection, a virtual private gateway provides two VPN endpoints (tunnels) for automatic failover. You configure your customer gateway on the remote side of the VPN connection. If you have more than one remote network (for example, multiple branch offices), you can create multiple AWS managed VPN connections via your virtual private gateway to enable communication between these networks.

You can create a VPN connection to your remote network by using an Amazon EC2 instance in your VPC that's running a third party software VPN appliance. AWS does not provide nor maintain third party software VPN appliances; however, you can choose from a range of products provided by partners and open source communities.

Option A is incorrect because it is not entirely true. Take note that AWS extends to its customers the responsibility of securing the cloud, which is called the 'Shared Responsibility Model'. AWS handles the security OF the cloud, while you manage the security IN the cloud.

Option C is incorrect. Having a VPN connection does not change the limits on the number of AWS resources you can provision.

Option D is incorrect because there is a way to connect your AWS cloud resources to on-premises data centers using VPN connections.

Reference:
http://docs.aws.amazon.com/AmazonVPC/latest/UserGuide/vpn-connections.html

QUESTION 4:

You are the Solutions Architect for your company's AWS account of approximately 300 IAM users. They have a new company policy that will change the access of 100 of the IAM users to have a particular sort of access to Amazon S3 buckets.

What will you do to avoid the time-consuming task of applying the policy at the individual user?

A. Create a new IAM group and then add the users that require access to the S3 bucket. Afterwards, apply the policy to IAM group. **(Correct)**

B. Create a new policy and apply it to multiple IAM users using a shell script.

C. Create a new S3 bucket access policy with unlimited access for each IAM user.

D. Create a new IAM role and add each user to the IAM role.

EXPLANATION

In this scenario, the best option is to group the set of users in an IAM Group and then apply a policy with the required access to the Amazon S3 bucket. This will enable you to easily add, remove, and manage the users instead of manually adding a policy to each and every 100 IAM users.

Option B is incorrect because you need a new IAM Group for this scenario and not assign a policy to each user via a shell script. This method can save you time but afterwards, it will be difficult to manage all 100 users that are not contained in an IAM Group.

Option C is incorrect because you need a new IAM Group and the method is also time-consuming.

Option D is incorrect because you need to use an IAM Group and not an IAM role.

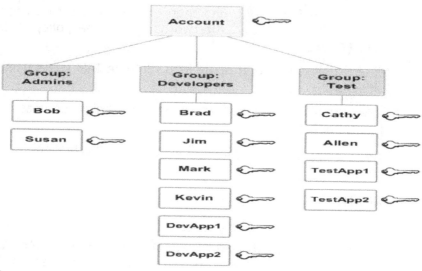

Reference:

http://docs.aws.amazon.com/IAM/latest/UserGuide/id_groups.html

QUESTION 5:

You are a Solutions Architect for a global news company. You are configuring a fleet of EC2 instances in a subnet which currently is in a VPC with an Internet gateway attached. All of these EC2 instances can be accessed from the Internet. You then launch another subnet and launch an EC2 instance in it, however you are not able to access the EC2 instance from the Internet.

What could be the possible reasons for this issue? (Choose 2)

A. The Amazon EC2 instance does not have a public IP address associated with it. **(Correct)**

B. The Amazon EC2 instance is not a member of the same Auto Scaling group.

C. The Amazon EC2 instance is running in an Availability Zone that does not support Internet access.

D. The route table is not configured properly to send traffic from the EC2 instance to the Internet through the Internet gateway. **(Correct)**

E. The route table is not configured properly to send traffic from the EC2 instance to the Internet through the customer gateway (CGW).

EXPLANATION

In cases where your EC2 instance cannot access the Internet, you usually have to check two things:

1. Does it have an EIP or public IP address?
2. Is the route table properly configured?

Below are the correct answers:

1. Amazon EC2 instance does not have a public IP address associated with it.
2. The route table is not configured properly to send traffic from the EC2 instance to the Internet through the Internet gateway.

Option B is incorrect since Auto Scaling Groups do not affect Internet connectivity of EC2 instances.

Option C is incorrect since there is no such Availability Zone where it does not specifically support Internet connectivity.

Option E is incorrect since CGW is used when you are setting up a VPN. The correct gateway should be an Internet gateway.

Reference:
http://docs.aws.amazon.com/AmazonVPC/latest/UserGuide/VPC_Scenario2.html

QUESTION 6:

You are working for a data analytics company as a Software Engineer, which has a client that is setting up an innovative checkout-free grocery store. You developed a monitoring application that uses smart sensors to collect the items that your customers are getting from the grocery's refrigerators and shelves then automatically maps it to their accounts. To know more about the buying behavior of your customers, you want to analyze the items that are constantly being bought and store the results in S3 for durable storage.

What service can you use to easily capture, transform, and load streaming data into Amazon S3, Amazon Elasticsearch Service, and Splunk?

A. Amazon Kinesis Data Firehose **(Correct)**

B. Amazon Kinesis

C. Amazon Redshift

D. Amazon Macie

EXPLANATION

Amazon Kinesis Data Firehose is the easiest way to load streaming data into data stores and analytics tools. It can capture, transform, and load streaming data into Amazon S3, Amazon Redshift, Amazon Elasticsearch Service, and Splunk, enabling near real-time analytics with existing business intelligence tools and dashboards you are already using today.

It is a fully managed service that automatically scales to match the throughput of your data and requires no ongoing administration. It can also batch, compress, and encrypt the data before loading it, minimizing the amount of storage used at the destination and increasing security.

In the diagram below, you gather the data from your smart refrigerators and use Kinesis Data firehouse to prepare and load the data. S3 will be used as a method of durably storing the data for analytics and the eventual ingestion of data for output using analytical tools.

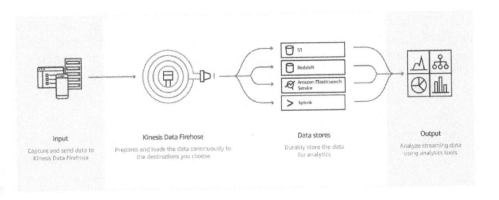

Option B is incorrect because Amazon Kinesis is the streaming data platform of AWS and has four distinct services under it: Kinesis Data Firehose, Kinesis Data Streams, Kinesis Video Streams, and Amazon Kinesis Data Analytics. For a specific use case of the requirement by the question, use Kinesis Data Firehose.

Option C is incorrect because Amazon Redshift is mainly used for data warehousing making it simple and cost-effective to analyze your data across your data warehouse and data lake. It does not meet the requirement of being able to load and stream data into data stores for analytics. You have to use Kinesis Data Firehose instead.

Option D is incorrect because Amazon Macie is mainly used as a security service that uses machine learning to automatically discover, classify, and protect sensitive data in AWS. As a security feature of AWS, it does not meet the requirements of being able to load and stream data into data stores for analytics. You have to use Kinesis Data Firehose instead.

Reference:
https://aws.amazon.com/kinesis/data-firehose/

QUESTION 7:

A large financial company has recently adopted a hybrid cloud architecture to integrate their on-premises data center and their AWS Cloud. Your manager has instructed you to create a new VPC network topology which must support all Internet-facing web applications as well as the internally-facing applications that is accessed by employees only over VPN. To ensure high-availability and fault tolerance, both of their Internet-facing and internally-facing financial applications must be able to leverage at least two AZs for high availability.

What is the minimum number of subnets that you must create within your VPC to accommodate these requirements?

A. 1 subnet

B. 2 subnets

C. 3 subnets

D. 4 subnets **(Correct)**

EXPLANATION

In this scenario, the requirement is to have at least 2 Availability Zones for both Internet-facing (public) and Internally-facing (private) applications. Remember that one subnet is mapped into one specific Availability Zone. Since we need to have at least 2 public and 2 private subnets, the correct answer is 4 subnets.

Amazon Web Services

A VPC spans all the Availability Zones in the region. After creating a VPC, you can add one or more subnets in each Availability Zone. When you create a subnet, you specify the CIDR block for the subnet, which is a subset of the VPC CIDR block. Each subnet must reside entirely within one Availability Zone and cannot span zones. Availability Zones are distinct locations that are engineered to be isolated from failures in other Availability Zones. By launching instances in separate Availability Zones, you can protect your applications from the failure of a single location. AWS assigns a unique ID to each subnet.

Reference:
https://docs.aws.amazon.com/AWSEC2/latest/UserGuide/using-regions availability-zones.html

QUESTION 8:

A manufacturing company has EC2 instances running in AWS. The EC2 instances are configured with Auto Scaling. There are a lot of requests being lost because of too much load on the servers. The Auto Scaling is launching new EC2 instances to take the load accordingly yet, there are still some requests that are being lost.

Which of the following is the most cost-effective solution to avoid losing recently submitted requests?

A. Use an SQS queue to decouple the application components **(Correct)**

B. Keep one extra Spot EC2 instance always ready in case a spike occurs.

C. Use larger instances for your application

D. Pre-warm your Elastic Load Balancer

EXPLANATION

In this scenario, Amazon SQS is the best solution to avoid having lost messages.

Amazon Simple Queue Service (SQS) is a fully managed message queuing service that makes it easy to decouple and scale microservices, distributed systems, and serverless applications. Building applications from individual components that each perform a discrete function improves scalability and reliability, and is best practice design for modern applications. SQS makes it simple and cost-effective to decouple and coordinate the components of a cloud application. Using SQS, you can send, store, and receive messages between software components at any volume, without losing messages or requiring other services to be always available.

Options B and C are wrong because using a Spot or a larger EC2 instance would not prevent data from being lost in case of a larger spike. You can take advantage of the durability and elasticity of SQS to keep the messages available for consumption by your instances.

Option D is incorrect because it would be difficult to predict how much traffic your load balancer will be receiving in a certain period of time, which corresponds to how long you will pre-warm the load balancer. It is still better to use SQS in this scenario rather than re-configuring your load balancer.

Reference:
https://aws.amazon.com/sqs/

QUESTION 9:

You have an On-Demand EC2 instance located in a subnet in AWS which hosts a web application. The security group attached to this EC2 instance has the following Inbound Rules:

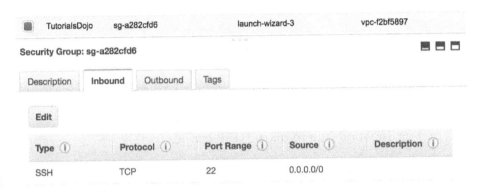

| TutorialsDojo | sg-a282cfd6 | launch-wizard-3 | | vpc-f2bf5897 |

Security Group: sg-a282cfd6

Description | **Inbound** | Outbound | Tags

Edit

Type ⓘ	Protocol ⓘ	Port Range ⓘ	Source ⓘ	Description ⓘ
SSH	TCP	22	0.0.0.0/0	

The Route table attached to the VPC is shown below. You can establish an SSH connection into the EC2 instance from the internet. However, you are not able to connect to the web server using your Chrome browser.

| TutorialsDojo | rtb-46b1813b | 0 Subnets | Yes | vpc-b0968fc8 |

rtb-46b1813b | TutorialsDojo

Summary | **Routes** | Subnet Associations | Route Propagation | Tags

Edit

View: All rules

Destination	Target	Status	Propagated
10.0.0.0/27	local	Active	No
0.0.0.0/0	igw-b51618cc	Active	No

Which of the below steps would resolve the issue?

A. In the Security Group, add an Inbound HTTP rule. **(Correct)**

B. In the Security Group, remove the SSH rule.

C. In the Route table, add this new route entry: 0.0.0.0 -> igw-b51618cc

D. In the Route table, add this new route entry: 10.0.0.0/27 -> local

EXPLANATION

The scenario is that you can already connect to the EC2 instance via SSH. This means that there is no problem in the Route Table of your VPC. To fix this issue, you simply need to update your Security Group and add an Inbound rule to allow HTTP traffic.

Option B is incorrect as removing the SSH rule will not solve the issue. It will just disable SSH traffic that is already available.

Options C and D are incorrect as there is no need to change the Route Tables.

Reference:
http://docs.aws.amazon.com/AmazonVPC/latest/UserGuide/VPC_SecurityGroups.html

QUESTION 10:

You are working for a startup as its AWS Chief Architect. You are currently assigned on a project that develops an online registration platform for events, which uses Simple Workflow for complete control of your orchestration logic. A decider ingests the customer name, address, contact number, and email address while the activity workers update the customer with the status of their online application status via email. Recently, you were having problems with your online registration platform which was solved by checking the decision task of your workflow.

In SWF, what is the purpose of a decision task?

A. It defines all the activities in the workflow.
B. It tells the decider the state of the workflow execution. **(Correct)**
C. It tells the worker to perform a function.
D. It represents a single task in the workflow.

EXPLANATION

Option B is correct. The decider can be viewed as a special type of worker. Like workers, it can be written in any language and asks Amazon SWF for tasks. However, it handles special tasks called decision tasks.

Amazon SWF issues decision tasks whenever a workflow execution has transitions such as an activity task completing or timing out. A decision task contains information on the inputs, outputs, and current state of previously initiated activity tasks. Your decider uses this data to decide the next steps, including any new activity tasks, and returns those to Amazon SWF. Amazon SWF in turn enacts these decisions, initiating new activity tasks where appropriate and monitoring them.

By responding to decision tasks in an ongoing manner, the decider controls the order, timing, and concurrency of activity tasks and consequently the execution of processing steps in the application. SWF issues the first decision task when an execution starts. From there on, Amazon SWF enacts the decisions made by your decider to drive your execution. The execution continues until your decider makes a decision to complete it.

Option A is incorrect because this is the definition of a workflow in SWF.
Option C is incorrect because this is the definition of an activity task.
Option D is incorrect because this is the definition of an SWF task.

References:

https://aws.amazon.com/swf/faqs/

http://docs.aws.amazon.com/amazonswf/latest/developerguide/swf-dg-dev-deciders.html

QUESTION 11:

You are a Solutions Architect in your company where you are tasked to set up a cloud infrastructure. In the planning, it was discussed that you will need two EC2 instances which should continuously run for three years. The CPU utilization of the EC2 instances is also expected to be stable and predictable.

Which is the most cost-efficient Amazon EC2 Pricing type that is most appropriate for this scenario?

A. Reserved Instances **(Correct)**

B. On-Demand instances

C. Spot instances

D. Dedicated Hosts

EXPLANATION

Reserved Instances provide you with a significant discount (up to 75%) compared to On-Demand instance pricing. In addition, when Reserved Instances are assigned to a specific Availability Zone, they provide a capacity reservation, giving you additional confidence in your ability to launch instances when you need them.

For applications that have steady state or predictable usage, Reserved Instances can provide significant savings compared to using On-Demand instances.

Reserved Instances are recommended for:
-Applications with steady state usage

-Applications that may require reserved capacity
-Customers that can commit to using EC2 over a 1 or 3 year term to reduce their total computing costs

References:

https://aws.amazon.com/ec2/pricing/

https://aws.amazon.com/ec2/pricing/reserved-instances/

QUESTION 12:

You are working as a Solutions Architect for an aerospace manufacturer which heavily uses AWS. They are running a cluster of multi-tier applications that spans multiple servers for your wind simulation model and how it affects your state-of-the-art wing design. Currently, you are experiencing a slowdown in your applications and upon further investigation, it was discovered that it is due to latency issues.

Which of the following EC2 features should you use to optimize performance for a compute cluster that requires low network latency?

A. Multiple Availability Zones

B. AWS Direct Connect

C. EC2 Dedicated Instances

D. Placement Groups **(Correct)**

EXPLANATION

You can launch EC2 instances in a placement group, which determines how instances are placed on underlying hardware. When you create a placement group, you specify one of the following strategies for the group:

1. **Cluster** - clusters instances into a low-latency group in a single Availability Zone
2. **Spread** - spreads instances across underlying hardware

Option A is incorrect because multiple availability zones are mainly used for achieving high availability when one of the AWS AZ's goes down, and are not used for low network latency. Use Spread Placement Groups instead for multiple availability zones.

Option B is incorrect because Direct Connect bypasses the public Internet and establishes a secure, dedicated connection from your on-premises data center into AWS, and not for having low latency within your AWS network. Use Placement Groups instead for low network latency.

Option C is incorrect because EC2 Dedicated Instances are EC2 instances that run in a VPC on hardware that is dedicated to a single customer and are physically isolated at the host hardware level from instances that belong to other AWS accounts. It is not used for reducing latency.

Reference:
http://docs.aws.amazon.com/AWSEC2/latest/UserGuide/placement-groups.html

QUESTION 13:

You installed sensors to track the number of visitors that goes to the park. The data is sent everyday to an Amazon Kinesis stream with default settings for processing, in which a consumer is configured to process the data every other day. You noticed that your S3 bucket is not receiving all of the data that is being sent to the Kinesis stream. You checked the sensors if they are properly sending the data to Amazon Kinesis and verified that the data is indeed sent everyday.

What could be the reason for this?

A. There is a problem in the sensors. They probably had some intermittent connection hence, the data is not sent to the stream.

B. By default, Amazon S3 stores the data for 1 day and moves it to Amazon Glacier.

C. Your AWS account was hacked and someone has deleted some data in your Kinesis stream.

D. By default, the data records are only accessible for 24 hours from the time they are added to a Kinesis stream. **(Correct)**

EXPLANATION

Kinesis Data Streams supports changes to the data record retention period of your stream. A Kinesis data stream is an ordered sequence of data records meant to be written to and read from in real-time. Data records are therefore stored in shards in your stream temporarily.

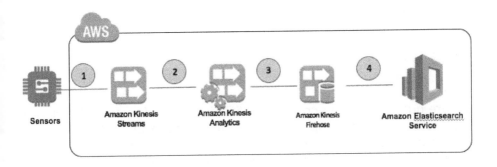

The time period from when a record is added to when it is no longer accessible is called the retention period. A Kinesis data stream stores records from 24 hours by default to a maximum of 168 hours.

This is the reason why there are missing data in your S3 bucket. To fix this, you can either configure your sensors to send the data everyday instead of every other day or alternatively, you can increase the retention period of your Kinesis data stream.

Option A is incorrect. You already verified that the sensors are working as they should be hence, this is not the root cause of the issue.

Option B is incorrect because by default, Amazon S3 does not store the data for 1 day and moves it to Amazon Glacier.

Option C is incorrect because although this could be a possibility, you should verify first if there are other more probable reasons for the missing data in your S3 bucket. Be sure to follow and apply security best practices as well to prevent being hacked by someone. By default, the data records are only accessible for 24 hours from the time they are added to a Kinesis stream and hence, Option D depicts the root cause of this issue and not Option C.

Reference:

http://docs.aws.amazon.com/streams/latest/dev/kinesis-extended-retention.html

QUESTION 14:

You are automating the creation of EC2 instances in your VPC. Hence, you wrote a python script to trigger the Amazon EC2 API to request 50 EC2 instances in a single Availability Zone. However, you noticed that after 20 successful requests, subsequent requests failed.

What could be a reason for this issue and how would you resolve it?

A. There was an issue with the Amazon EC2 API. Just resend the requests and these will be provisioned successfully.

B. By default, AWS allows you to provision a maximum of 20 instances per region. Select a different region and retry the failed request.

C. By default, AWS allows you to provision a maximum of 20 instances per Availability Zone. Select a different Availability Zone and retry the failed request.

D. There is a soft limit of 20 instances per region which is why subsequent requests failed. Just submit the limit increase form to AWS and retry the failed requests once approved. **(Correct)**

EXPLANATION

You are limited to running up to a total of 20 On-Demand instances across the instance family, purchasing 20 Reserved Instances and requesting Spot Instances per your dynamic Spot limit per region. If you wish to run more than 20 instances, complete the Amazon EC2 instance request form.

Option A is incorrect. There is a soft limit of 20 instances that you can provision per region, which is why only 20 instances were started.

Option B is incorrect. There is no need to select a different region since this limit can be increased after submitting a request form to AWS.

Option C is incorrect because the maximum of 20 instances limit is set per region and not per Availability Zone. This can be increased after submitting a request form to AWS.

References:

https://docs.aws.amazon.com/general/latest/gr/aws_service_limits.html#limits_ec2

https://aws.amazon.com/ec2/faqs/#How_many_instances_can_I_run_in_Amazon_EC2

QUESTION 15:

You are working as an IT Consultant for a large investment bank that generates large financial datasets with millions of rows. The data must be stored in a columnar fashion to reduce the number of disk I/O requests and reduce the amount of data needed to load from the disk. The bank has an existing third-party business intelligence application which will connect to the storage service and then generate daily and monthly financial reports for its clients around the globe.

In this scenario, which is the best storage service to use to meet the requirement?

A. Amazon Redshift **(Correct)**

B. Amazon RDS

C. Amazon Aurora

D. DynamoDB

EXPLANATION

Amazon Redshift is a fast, scalable data warehouse that makes it simple and cost-effective to analyze all your data across your data warehouse and data lake. Redshift delivers ten times faster performance than other data warehouses by using machine learning, massively parallel query execution, and columnar storage on high-performance disk.

In this scenario, there is a requirement to have a storage service which will be used by a business intelligence application and where the data must be stored in a columnar fashion. Business Intelligence reporting systems is a type of Online Analytical Processing (OLAP) which Redshift is known to support. In addition, Redshift also provides columnar storage unlike the other options. Hence, the correct answer in this scenario is Option A: Amazon Redshift.

References:

https://docs.aws.amazon.com/redshift/latest/dg/c_columnar_storage _disk_mem_mgmnt.html

https://aws.amazon.com/redshift/

Here is a case study on finding the most suitable analytical tool - Kinesis vs EMR vs Athena vs Redshift:

https://youtu.be/wEOm6aiN4ww

QUESTION 16:

A global online sports betting company has its popular web application hosted in AWS. They are planning to develop a new online portal for their new business venture and they hired you to implement the cloud architecture for a new online portal that will accept bets globally for world sports. You started to design the system with a relational database that runs on a single EC2 instance, which requires a single EBS volume that can support up to 30,000 IOPS.

In this scenario, which Amazon EBS volume type can you use that will meet the performance requirements of this new online portal?

   A. EBS Provisioned IOPS SSD (io1) **(Correct)**

   B. EBS Throughput Optimized HDD (st1)

   C. EBS General Purpose SSD (gp2)

   D. EBS Cold HDD (sc1)

EXPLANATION

The scenario requires a storage type for a relational database with a high IOPS performance. For these scenarios, SSD volumes are more suitable to use instead of HDD volumes. Remember that the dominant performance attribute of SSD is IOPS while HDD is Throughput.

In the exam, always consider the difference between SSD and HDD as shown on the table below. This will allow you to easily eliminate specific EBS-types in the options which are not SSD or not HDD, depending on whether the Question asks for a storage type which has small, random I/O operations or large, sequential I/O operations.

Since the requirement is 30,000 IOPS, you have to use an EBS type of Provisioned IOPS SSD, as this type can handle a maximum of 32,000 IOPS. This provides sustained performance for mission-critical low-latency workloads. Hence, Option A is the correct answer.

Options B and D are incorrect because these are HDD volumes which are more suitable for large streaming workloads rather than transactional database workloads.

Option C is incorrect because although a General Purpose SSD volume can be used for this scenario, it does not provide the high IOPS required by the application, unlike the Provisioned IOPS SSD volume.

Reference:
https://aws.amazon.com/ebs/details/

FEATURES	SSD Solid State Drive	HDD Hard Disk Drive
Best for workloads with:	*small, random* I/O operations	*large, sequential* I/O operations
Can be used as a bootable volume?	Yes	No
Suitable Use Cases	– Best for transactional workloads – Critical business applications that require sustained IOPS performance – Large database workloads such as MongoDB, Oracle, Microsoft SQL Server and many others…	– Best for *large streaming workloads* requiring consistent, fast throughput at a low price – Big data, Data warehouses, Log processing – Throughput-oriented storage for large volumes of data that is *infrequently* accessed
Cost	moderate / high	low
Dominant Performance Attribute	IOPS	Throughput (MiB/s)

QUESTION 17:

A large insurance company has an AWS account that contains three VPCs (DEV, UAT and PROD) in the same region. UAT is peered to both PROD and DEV using a VPC peering connection. All VPCs have non-overlapping CIDR blocks. The company wants to push minor code releases from Dev to Prod to speed up time to market.

Which of the following options helps the company accomplish this?

A. Create a new VPC peering connection between PROD and DEV with the appropriate routes. **(Correct)**

B. Create a new entry to PROD in the DEV route table using the VPC peering connection as the target.

C. Change the DEV and PROD VPCs to have overlapping CIDR blocks to be able to connect them.

D. Do nothing. Since these two VPCs are already connected via UAT, they already have a connection to each other.

EXPLANATION

A VPC peering connection is a networking connection between two VPCs that enables you to route traffic between them privately. Instances in either VPC can communicate with each other as if they are within the same network. You can create a VPC peering connection between your own VPCs, with a VPC in another AWS account, or with a VPC in a different AWS Region.

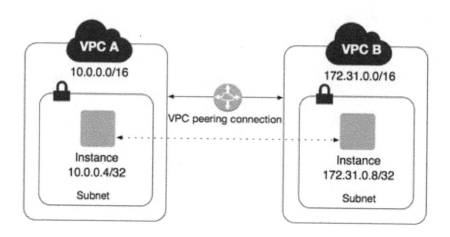

AWS uses the existing infrastructure of a VPC to create a VPC peering connection; it is neither a gateway nor a VPN connection and does not rely on a separate piece of physical hardware. There is no single point of failure for communication or a bandwidth bottleneck.

Option B is incorrect because even if you configure the route tables, the two VPCs will still be disconnected until you set up a VPC peering connection between them.

Option C is incorrect because you cannot peer two VPCs with overlapping CIDR blocks.

Option D is incorrect as transitive VPC peering is not allowed hence, even though DEV and PROD are both connected in UAT, these two VPCs do not have a direct connection to each other.

Reference:

https://docs.aws.amazon.com/AmazonVPC/latest/UserGuide/vpc-peering.html

Here is a quick introduction to VPC Peering:

https://youtu.be/i1A1eH8vLtk

QUESTION 18:

You are working for an insurance firm as their Senior Solutions Architect. The firm has an application which processes thousands of customer data stored in an Amazon MySQL database with Multi-AZ deployments configuration for high availability in case of downtime. For the past few days, you noticed an increasing trend of read and write operations, which is increasing the latency of the queries to your database. You are planning to use the standby database instance to balance the read and write operations from the primary instance.

When running your primary Amazon RDS Instance as a Multi-AZ deployment, can you use the standby instance for read and write operations?

A. Yes

B. Only with Microsoft SQL Server-based RDS

C. Only for Oracle RDS instances

D. No **(Correct)**

EXPLANATION

The answer is No. The standby instance will not perform any read and write operations while the primary instance is running. Hence, Option D is the correct answer.

Multi-AZ deployments for the MySQL, MariaDB, Oracle, and PostgreSQL engines utilize synchronous physical replication to keep data on the standby up-to-date with the primary. Multi-AZ deployments for the SQL Server engine use synchronous logical replication to achieve the same result, employing SQL Server-native Mirroring technology. Both approaches safeguard your data in the event of a DB Instance failure or loss of an Availability Zone.

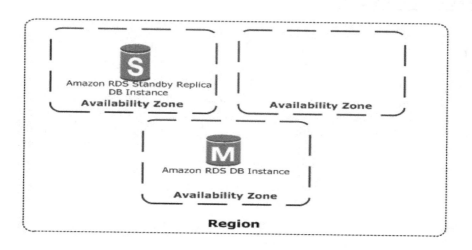

If a storage volume on your primary instance fails in a Multi-AZ deployment, Amazon RDS automatically initiates a failover to the up-to-date standby (or to a replica in the case of Amazon Aurora). Compare this to a Single-AZ deployment: in case of a Single-AZ database failure, a user-initiated point-in-time-restore operation will be required. This operation can take several hours to complete, and any data updates that occurred after the latest restorable time (typically within the last five minutes) will not be available.

Options A, B and C are incorrect because, regardless of the database engine, you cannot use a standby database for read and write operations.

Reference:

QUESTION 19:

A music company is storing data on Amazon Simple Storage Service (S3). The company's security policy requires that data are encrypted at rest. Which of the following methods can achieve this? (Choose 2)

E. Use SSL to encrypt the data while in transit to Amazon S3.

F. Use Amazon S3 server-side encryption with customer-provided keys. **(Correct)**

G. Use Amazon S3 bucket policies to restrict access to the data at rest.

H. Use Amazon S3 server-side encryption with EC2 key pair.

I. Encrypt the data on the client-side before ingesting to Amazon S3 using their own master key. **(Correct)**

EXPLANATION

Data protection refers to protecting data while in-transit (as it travels to and from Amazon S3) and at rest (while it is stored on disks in Amazon S3 data centers). You can protect data in transit by using SSL or by using client-side encryption. You have the following options for protecting data at rest in Amazon S3:

Use Server-Side Encryption – You request Amazon S3 to encrypt your object before saving it on disks in its data centers and decrypt it when you download the objects.

1. Use Server-Side Encryption with Amazon S3-Managed Keys (SSE-S3)

2. Use Server-Side Encryption with AWS KMS-Managed Keys (SSE-KMS)

3. Use Server-Side Encryption with Customer-Provided Keys (SSE-C)

Use Client-Side Encryption – You can encrypt data client-side and upload the encrypted data to Amazon S3. In this case, you manage the encryption process, the encryption keys, and related tools.

1. Use Client-Side Encryption with AWS KMS–Managed Customer Master Key (CMK)
2. Use Client-Side Encryption Using a Client-Side Master Key

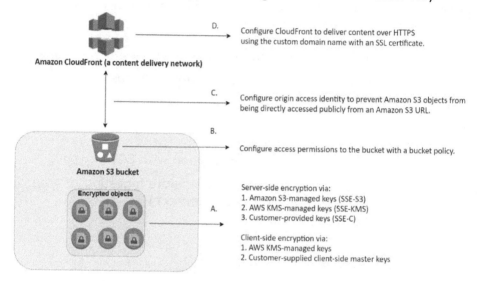

Reference:

http://docs.aws.amazon.com/AmazonS3/latest/dev/UsingEncryption.html

QUESTION 20:

You are working for an investment bank as their IT Consultant. You are working with their IT team to handle the launch of their digital wallet system. The applications will run on multiple EBS-backed EC2 instances which will store the logs, transactions, and billing statements of the user in an S3 bucket. Due to tight security and compliance requirements, you are exploring options on how to safely store sensitive data on the EBS volumes and S3.

Which of the below options should be carried out on AWS when storing sensitive data? (Choose 2)

A. Create an EBS Snapshot

B. Enable EBS Encryption **(Correct)**

C. Migrate the EC2 instances from the public to private subnet.

D. Enable Amazon S3 Server-Side and Client-Side Encryption **(Correct)**

E. Use AWS Shield and WAF

EXPLANATION

Both Options B and D are correct. Amazon EBS encryption offers a simple encryption solution for your EBS volumes without the need to build, maintain, and secure your own key management infrastructure.

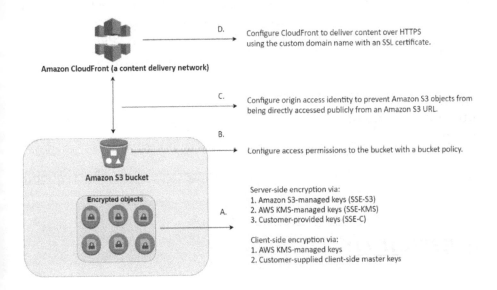

In Amazon S3, data protection refers to protecting data while in-transit (as it travels to and from Amazon S3) and at rest (while it is stored on disks in Amazon S3 data centers). You can protect data in transit by using SSL or by using client-side encryption. You have the following options to protect data at rest in Amazon S3.

Use Server-Side Encryption – You request Amazon S3 to encrypt your object before saving it on disks in its data centers and decrypt it when you download the objects.

Use Client-Side Encryption – You can encrypt data client-side and upload the encrypted data to Amazon S3. In this case, you manage the encryption process, the encryption keys, and related tools.

Option A is incorrect because taking EBS Snapshot is a backup solution of EBS. It does not provide security of data inside EBS volumes when executed.

Option C is incorrect because the data you want to secure are those in EBS volumes and S3 buckets. Moving your EC2 instance to a private subnet involves a different matter of security practice, which does not achieve what you want in this scenario.

Option E is incorrect because Shield and WAF protect you from common security threats for your web applications. However, what you are trying to achieve is securing and encrypting your data inside EBS and S3.

References:
http://docs.aws.amazon.com/AWSEC2/latest/UserGuide/EBSEncryptio n.html

http://docs.aws.amazon.com/AmazonS3/latest/dev/UsingEncryption.h tml

QUESTION 21:

A document sharing website is using AWS as its cloud infrastructure. Free users can upload a total of 5 GB data while premium users can upload as much as 5 TB. Their application uploads the user files, which can have a max file size of 1 TB, to an S3 Bucket.

In this scenario, what is the best way for the application to upload the large files in S3?

A. Use a single PUT request to upload the large file

B. Use Amazon Snowball

C. Use AWS Import/Export

D. Use Multipart Upload **(Correct)**

EXPLANATION

The total volume of data and number of objects you can store are unlimited. Individual Amazon S3 objects can range in size from a minimum of 0 bytes to a maximum of 5 terabytes. The largest object that can be uploaded in a single PUT is 5 gigabytes. For objects larger than 100 megabytes, customers should consider using the Multipart Upload capability.

The Multipart upload API enables you to upload large objects in parts. You can use this API to upload new large objects or make a copy of an existing object. Multipart uploading is a three-step process: you initiate the upload, you upload the object parts, and after you have uploaded all the parts, you complete the multipart upload. Upon receiving the complete multipart upload request, Amazon S3 constructs the object from the uploaded parts and you can then access the object just as you would any other object in your bucket.

Option A is incorrect because the largest file size you can upload using a single PUT request is 5 GB. Files larger than this will fail to be uploaded.

Option B is incorrect because Snowball is a migration tool that lets you transfer large amounts of data from your on-premises data center to AWS S3 and vice versa. This tool is not suitable for the given scenario. And when you provision Snowball, the device gets transported to you, and not to your customers. Therefore, you bear the responsibility of securing the device.

Option C is incorrect because Import/Export is similar to AWS Snowball in such a way that it is meant to be used as a migration tool, and not for multiple customer consumption such as in the given scenario.

References:

https://docs.aws.amazon.com/AmazonS3/latest/dev/mpuoverview.html

https://aws.amazon.com/s3/faqs/

QUESTION 22:

An Architect is managing a data analytics application which exclusively uses Amazon S3 as its data storage. For the past few weeks, the application works as expected until a new change was implemented to increase the rate at which the application updates its data. There have been reports that outdated data intermittently appears when the application accesses objects from S3 bucket. The development team investigated the application logic and didn't find any issues.

Which of the following is the MOST likely cause of this issue?

A. The data analytics application is designed to fetch parts of objects from the S3 bucket using a range header.

B. The data analytics application is designed to fetch objects from the S3 bucket using parallel requests. **(Correct)**

C. The data analytics application is designed to use atomic updates across object keys.

D. The data analytics application is designed to update its data with an object-locking mechanism.

EXPLANATION

Amazon S3 provides read-after-write consistency for PUTS of new objects in your S3 bucket in all regions with one caveat: if you make a HEAD or GET request to the key name (to find if the object exists) before creating the object, Amazon S3 provides eventual consistency for read-after-write. Amazon S3 offers eventual consistency for overwrite PUTS and DELETES in all regions.

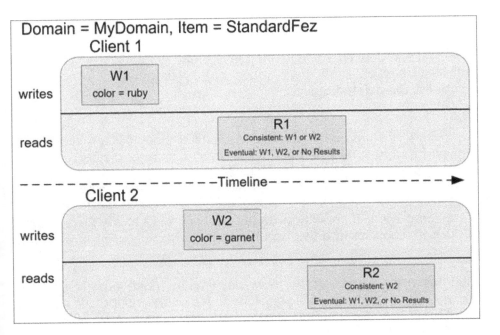

Updates to a single key are atomic. For example, if you PUT to an existing key, a subsequent read might return the old data or the updated data, but it will never return corrupted or partial data. This usually happens if your application is using parallel requests on the same object.

Amazon S3 achieves high availability by replicating data across multiple servers within Amazon's data centers. If a PUT request is successful, your data is safely stored. However, information about the changes must replicate across Amazon S3, which can take some time, and so you might observe the following behaviors:

- A process writes a new object to Amazon S3 and immediately lists keys within its bucket. Until the change is fully propagated, the object might not appear in the list.

- A process replaces an existing object and immediately attempts to read it. Until the change is fully propagated, Amazon S3 might return the prior data.

- A process deletes an existing object and immediately attempts to read it. Until the deletion is fully propagated, Amazon S3 might return the deleted data.

- A process deletes an existing object and immediately lists keys within its bucket. Until the deletion is fully propagated, Amazon S3 might list the deleted object.

Amazon S3's support for parallel requests means you can scale your S3 performance by the factor of your compute cluster, without making any customizations to your application. Amazon S3 does not currently support Object Locking. If two PUT requests are simultaneously made to the same key, the request with the latest timestamp wins. If this is an issue, you will need to build an object-locking mechanism into your application.

Updates are key-based; there is no way to make atomic updates across keys. For example, you cannot make the update of one key dependent on the update of another key unless you design this functionality into your application.

Hence, the correct answer is Option B.

Option A is incorrect because using a Range header is primarily used to retrieve an object in parts and is unlikely the root cause on why the application is intermittently getting old data. Using the Range HTTP header in a GET request, you can retrieve a specific range of bytes in an object stored in Amazon S3. With this, you can resume fetching other parts of the object whenever your application is ready. This resumable download is useful when you need only portions of your object data. It is also useful where network connectivity is poor and you need to react to failures.

Option C is incorrect because the update operations are key-based which means that there is no way to make atomic updates across keys. Hence, this is not the root cause of this issue.

Option D is incorrect because an object-locking mechanism will actually safeguard the application from the issue of getting obsolete data and not the other way around. Moreover, Amazon S3 does not currently support Object Locking.

References:
https://docs.aws.amazon.com/AmazonS3/latest/dev/Introduction.html
https://docs.aws.amazon.com/AmazonS3/latest/API/RESTObjectGET.html

QUESTION 23:

You are working for a Social Media Analytics company as its head data analyst. You want to collect gigabytes of data per second from websites and social media feeds to gain insights from data generated by its offerings and continuously improve the user experience. To meet this design requirement, you have developed an application hosted on an Auto Scaling group of Spot EC2 instances which processes the data and stores the results to DynamoDB and Redshift.

Which AWS service can you use to collect and process large streams of data records in real time?

A. Amazon S3

B. Amazon Redshift

C. Amazon SWF

D. Amazon Kinesis Data Streams **(Correct)**

EXPLANATION

Amazon Kinesis Data Streams is used to collect and process large streams of data records in real time. You can use Kinesis Data Streams for rapid and continuous data intake and aggregation. The type of data used includes IT infrastructure log data, application logs, social media, market data feeds, and web clickstream data. Because the response time for the data intake and processing is in real time, the processing is typically lightweight.

The following diagram illustrates the high-level architecture of Kinesis Data Streams. The producers continually push data to Kinesis Data Streams, and the consumers process the data in real time. Consumers (such as a custom application running on Amazon EC2 or an Amazon Kinesis Data Firehose delivery stream) can store their results using an AWS service such as Amazon DynamoDB, Amazon Redshift, or Amazon S3.

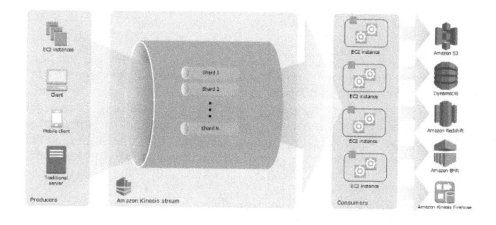

Option A is incorrect because S3 is mainly used for object storage of frequently and infrequently accessed files with high durability. It does not meet the requirement of being able to collect and process large streams of data in real time. You have to use Kinesis data streams instead.

Option B is incorrect because Amazon Redshift is mainly used for data warehousing making it simple and cost-effective to analyze your data across your data warehouse and data lake. Again, it does not meet the requirement of being able to collect and process large streams of data real time.

Option C is incorrect because SWF is mainly used to build applications that use Amazon's cloud to coordinate work across distributed components and not used as a way to process large streams of data records.

Reference:
https://docs.aws.amazon.com/streams/latest/dev/introduction.html

QUESTION 24:

You are working for a startup company that has resources deployed on the AWS Cloud. Your company is now going through a set of scheduled audits by an external auditing firm for compliance.

Which of the following services available in AWS can be utilized to help ensure the right information are present for auditing purposes?

A. AWS CloudTrail **(Correct)**

B. AWS VPC

C. AWS EC2

D. AWS Cloudwatch

EXPLANATION

AWS CloudTrail is a service that enables governance, compliance, operational auditing, and risk auditing of your AWS account. With CloudTrail, you can log, continuously monitor, and retain account activity related to actions across your AWS infrastructure. CloudTrail provides event history of your AWS account activity, including actions taken through the AWS Management Console, AWS SDKs, command line tools, and other AWS services. This event history simplifies security analysis, resource change tracking, and troubleshooting.

CloudTrail provides visibility into user activity by recording actions taken on your account. CloudTrail records important information about each action, including who made the request, the services used, the actions performed, parameters for the actions, and the response elements returned by the AWS service. This information helps you to track changes made to your AWS resources and troubleshoot operational issues. CloudTrail makes it easier to ensure compliance with internal policies and regulatory standards.

Option B is incorrect because a VPC is a logically isolated section of the AWS Cloud where you can launch AWS resources in a virtual network that you define. It does not provide you the auditing information that were asked for in this scenario.

Option C is incorrect because EC2 is a service that provides secure, resizable compute capacity in the cloud and does not provide the needed information in this scenario just like Option B.

Option D is incorrect because CloudWatch is a monitoring tool for your AWS resources. Like Options B and C, it does not provide the needed information to satisfy the requirement in the scenario.

Reference:
https://aws.amazon.com/cloudtrail/

QUESTION 25:

You are working for a FinTech startup as their AWS Solutions Architect. You deployed an application on different EC2 instances with Elastic IP addresses attached for easy DNS resolution and configuration. These servers are only accessed from 8 AM to 6 PM and can be stopped from 6 PM to 8 AM for cost efficiency using Lambda with the script that automates this based on tags.

Which of the following will occur when an EC2-VPC instance with an associated Elastic IP is stopped and started? (Choose 2)

A. The underlying host for the instance is possibly changed. **(Correct)**

B. The ENI (Elastic Network Interface) is detached.

C. All data on the attached instance-store devices will be lost. **(Correct)**

D. The Elastic IP address is disassociated with the instance.

E. There will be no changes.

EXPLANATION

This Question did not mention the specific type of EC2 instance however, it says that it will be stopped and started. Since only EBS-backed instances can be stopped and restarted, it is implied that the instance is EBS-backed. Remember that an instance store-backed instance can only be rebooted or terminated and its data will be erased if the EC2 instance is terminated.

If you stopped an EBS-backed EC2 instance, the volume is preserved but the data in any attached Instance store volumes will be erased. Keep in mind that an EC2 instance has an underlying physical host computer. If the instance is stopped, AWS usually moves the instance to a new host computer. Your instance may stay on the same host computer if there are no problems with the host computer. In addition, its Elastic IP address is disassociated from the instance if it is an EC2-Classic instance. Otherwise, if it is an EC2-VPC instance, the Elastic IP address remains associated.

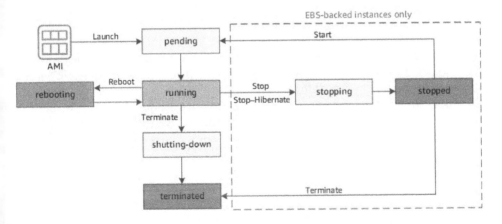

Reference:

http://docs.aws.amazon.com/AWSEC2/latest/UserGuide/ec2-instance-lifecycle.html

QUESTION 26:

You are working for a large IT consultancy company as a Solutions Architect. One of your clients is launching a file sharing web application in AWS which requires a durable storage service for hosting their static contents such as PDFs, Word Documents, high resolution images and many others.

Which type of storage service should you use to meet this requirement?

A. Amazon EBS volume

B. Amazon S3 **(Correct)**

C. Amazon EC2 instance store

D. Amazon RDS instance

EXPLANATION

Amazon S3 is storage for the Internet. It's a simple storage service that offers software developers a durable, highly-scalable, reliable, and low-latency data storage infrastructure at very low costs. Amazon S3 provides customers with a highly durable storage infrastructure. Versioning offers an additional level of protection by providing a means of recovery when customers accidentally overwrite or delete objects. Remember that the scenario requires a durable storage for static content. These two keywords are actually referring to S3, since it is highly durable and suitable for storing static content. Hence, Option B is correct.

Storage Need	Solution	AWS Services
Temporary storage	Consider using local instance store volumes for needs such as scratch disks, buffers, queues, and caches.	Amazon Local Instance Store
Multi-instance storage	Amazon EBS volumes can only be attached to one EC2 instance at a time. If you need multiple EC2 instances accessing volume data at the same time, consider using Amazon EFS as a file system.	Amazon EFS
Highly durable storage	If you need very highly durable storage, use S3 or Amazon EFS. Amazon S3 Standard storage is designed for 99.999999999 percent (11 nines) annual durability per object. You can even decide to take a snapshot of the EBS volumes. Such a snapshot then gets saved in Amazon S3, thus providing you the durability of Amazon S3. For more information on EBS durability, see the Durability and Availability section. EFS is designed for high durability and high availability, with data stored in multiple Availability Zones within an AWS Region.	Amazon S3 Amazon EFS
Static data or web content	If your data doesn't change that often, Amazon S3 might represent a more cost-effective and scalable solution for storing this fixed information. Also, web content served out of Amazon EBS requires a web server running on Amazon EC2; in contrast, you can deliver web content directly out of Amazon S3 or from multiple EC2 instances using Amazon EFS.	Amazon S3 Amazon EFS

Option A is incorrect because Amazon EBS volume is not as durable compared with S3. In addition, it is best to store the static contents in S3 rather than EBS.

Option C is incorrect because Amazon EC2 instance store is definitely not suitable - the data it holds will be wiped out immediately once the EC2 instance is restarted.

Option D is incorrect because an RDS instance is just a database and not suitable for storing static content. By default, RDS is not durable, unless you launch it to be in Multi-AZ deployments configuration.

Reference:

https://aws.amazon.com/s3/faqs/

https://d1.awsstatic.com/whitepapers/Storage/AWS%20Storage%20S ervices%20Whitepaper-v9.pdf#page=24

QUESTION 27:

An online stocks trading application that stores financial data in an S3 bucket has a lifecycle policy that moves older data to Glacier every month. There is a strict compliance requirement where a surprise audit can happen at anytime and you should be able to retrieve the required data in under 15 minutes under all circumstances. Your manager instructed you to ensure that retrieval capacity is available when you need it and should handle up to 150 MB/s of retrieval throughput.

Which of the following should you do to meet the above requirement? (Choose 2)

A. Retrieve the data using Amazon Glacier Select.

B. Use Expedited Retrieval to access the financial data. **(Correct)**

C. Use Bulk Retrieval to access the financial data.

D. Specify a range, or portion, of the financial data archive to retrieve.

E. Purchase provisioned retrieval capacity. **(Correct)**

EXPLANATION

Expedited retrievals allow you to quickly access your data when occasional urgent requests for a subset of archives are required. For all but the largest archives (250 MB+), data accessed using Expedited retrievals are typically made available within 1–5 minutes. Provisioned Capacity ensures that retrieval capacity for Expedited retrievals is available when you need it.

To make an Expedited, Standard, or Bulk retrieval, set the Tier parameter in the Initiate Job (POST jobs) REST API request to the option you want, or the equivalent in the AWS CLI or AWS SDKs. If you have purchased provisioned capacity, then all expedited retrievals are automatically served through your provisioned capacity.

Provisioned capacity ensures that your retrieval capacity for expedited retrievals is available when you need it. Each unit of capacity provides that at least three expedited retrievals can be performed every five minutes and provides up to 150 MB/s of retrieval throughput. You should purchase provisioned retrieval capacity if your workload requires highly reliable and predictable access to a subset of your data in minutes. Without provisioned capacity Expedited retrievals are accepted, except for rare situations of unusually high demand. However, if you require access to Expedited retrievals under all circumstances, you must purchase provisioned retrieval capacity.

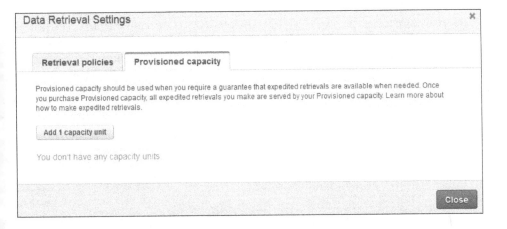

Option A is incorrect because Amazon Glacier Select is not an archive retrieval option and is primarily used to perform filtering operations using simple Structured Query Language (SQL) statements directly on your data archive in Glacier.

Option C is incorrect because Bulk retrievals typically complete within 5-12 hours hence, this does not satisfy the requirement of retrieving the data within 15 minutes. The provisioned capacity option is also not compatible with Bulk retrievals.

Option D is incorrect because using ranged archive retrievals is not enough to meet the requirement of retrieving the whole archive in the given timeframe. In addition, it does not provide additional retrieval capacity which is what the provisioned capacity option can offer.

References:

https://docs.aws.amazon.com/amazonglacier/latest/dev/downloading-an-archive-two-steps.html

https://docs.aws.amazon.com/amazonglacier/latest/dev/glacier-select.html

QUESTION 28:

You are working as an IT Consultant for a large media company where you are tasked to design a web application that stores static assets in an Amazon Simple Storage Service (S3) bucket. You expect this S3 bucket to immediately receive over 2000 PUT requests and 3500 GET requests per second at peak hour.

What should you do to ensure optimal performance?

- A. Use Amazon Glacier instead.
- B. Add a random prefix to the key names.
- C. Do nothing. Amazon S3 will automatically manage performance at this scale. **(Correct)**
- D. Use a predictable naming scheme in the key names such as sequential numbers or date time sequences.

EXPLANATION

Amazon S3 now provides increased performance to support at least 3,500 requests per second to add data and 5,500 requests per second to retrieve data, which can save significant processing time for no additional charge. Each S3 prefix can support these request rates, making it simple to increase performance significantly.

Applications running on Amazon S3 today will enjoy this performance improvement with no changes, and customers building new applications on S3 do not have to make any application customizations to achieve this performance. Amazon S3's support for parallel requests means you can scale your S3 performance by the factor of your compute cluster, without making any customizations to your application. Performance scales per prefix, so you can use as many prefixes as you need in parallel to achieve the required throughput. There are no limits to the number of prefixes.

This S3 request rate performance increase removes any previous guidance to randomize object prefixes to achieve faster performance. That means you can now use logical or sequential naming patterns in S3 object naming without any performance implications. This improvement is now available in all AWS Regions.

Option A is incorrect because it is an archival/long term storage solution, which is not optimal if you are serving objects frequently and fast retrieval is a must.

Option B is incorrect. Adding a random prefix is not required in this scenario because S3 can now scale automatically to adjust perfomance. You do not need to add a random prefix anymore for this purpose since S3 has increased performance to support at least 3,500 requests per second to add data and 5,500 requests per second to retrieve data, which covers the workload in the scenario.

Option D is incorrect because Amazon S3 already maintains an index of object key names in each AWS region. S3 stores key names in alphabetical order. The key name dictates which partition the key is stored in. Using a sequential prefix increases the likelihood that Amazon S3 will target a specific partition for a large number of your keys, overwhelming the I/O capacity of the partition.

References:

https://docs.aws.amazon.com/AmazonS3/latest/dev/request-rate-perf-considerations.html

https://aws.amazon.com/about-aws/whats-new/2018/07/amazon-s3-announces-increased-request-rate-performance/

QUESTION 29:

You are working as a Solutions Architect for a multinational financial firm. They have a global online trading platform in which the users from all over the world regularly upload terabytes of transactional data to a centralized S3 bucket. What AWS feature should you use in your present system to improve throughput and ensure consistently fast data transfer to the Amazon S3 bucket, regardless of your user's location?

A. FTP

B. AWS Direct Connect

C. Amazon S3 Transfer Acceleration **(Correct)**

D. Use CloudFront Origin Access Identity

EXPLANATION

Amazon S3 Transfer Acceleration enables fast, easy, and secure transfers of files over long distances between your client and your Amazon S3 bucket. Transfer Acceleration leverages Amazon CloudFront's globally distributed AWS Edge Locations. As data arrives at an AWS Edge Location, data is routed to your Amazon S3 bucket over an optimized network path.

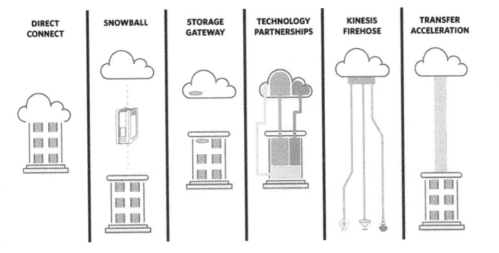

| DIRECT CONNECT | SNOWBALL | STORAGE GATEWAY | TECHNOLOGY PARTNERSHIPS | KINESIS FIREHOSE | TRANSFER ACCELERATION |

Option A is incorrect because the File Transfer Protocol does not guarantee fast throughput and consistent, fast data transfer.

Option B is incorrect because you have users all around the world and not just on your on-premises data center. Direct Connect would be too costly and is definitely not suitable for this purpose.

Option D is incorrect because this is a feature which ensures that only CloudFront can serve S3 content. It does not increase throughput and ensure fast delivery of content to your customers.

Reference:
http://docs.aws.amazon.com/AmazonS3/latest/dev/transfer-acceleration.html

QUESTION 30:

You are a new Solutions Architect working for a financial company. Your manager wants to have the ability to automatically transfer obsolete data from their S3 bucket to a low cost storage system in AWS.

What is the best solution you can provide to them?

A. Use an EC2 instance and a scheduled job to transfer the obsolete data from their S3 location to Amazon Glacier.

B. Use Lifecycle Policies in S3 to move obsolete data to Glacier. **(Correct)**

C. Use AWS SQS.

D. Use AWS SWF.

EXPLANATION

In this scenario, you can use lifecycle policies in S3 to automatically move obsolete data to Glacier.

Lifecycle configuration in Amazon S3 enables you to specify the lifecycle management of objects in a bucket. The configuration is a set of one or more rules, where each rule defines an action for Amazon S3 to apply to a group of objects. These actions can be classified as follows:

Transition actions – In which you define when objects transition to another storage class. For example, you may choose to transition objects to the STANDARD_IA (IA, for infrequent access) storage class 30 days after creation, or archive objects to the GLACIER storage class one year after creation.

Expiration actions – In which you specify when the objects expire. Then Amazon S3 deletes the expired objects on your behalf.

Option A is incorrect because you don't need to create a scheduled job in EC2 as you can just simply use the lifecycle policy in S3.

Options C and D are incorrect as SQS and SWF are not storage services.

References:

http://docs.aws.amazon.com/AmazonS3/latest/dev/object-lifecycle-mgmt.html

https://aws.amazon.com/blogs/aws/archive-s3-to-glacier/

QUESTION 31:

You are designing a social media website for a startup company and the founders want to know the ways to mitigate distributed denial-of-service (DDoS) attacks to their website.

Which of the following are not viable mitigation techniques? (Choose 2)

A. Use Dedicated EC2 instances to ensure that each instance has the maximum performance possible. **(Correct)**

B. Add multiple elastic network interfaces (ENIs) to each EC2 instance to increase the network bandwidth. **(Correct)**

C. Use an Amazon CloudFront service for distributing both static and dynamic content.

D. Use an Application Load Balancer with Auto Scaling groups for your EC2 instances then restrict direct Internet traffic to your Amazon RDS database by deploying to a private subnet.

E. Use AWS Shield and AWS WAF.

EXPLANATION

Take note that the Question asks about the viable mitigation techniques to avoid Distributed Denial of Service (DDoS) attack.

A Denial of Service (DoS) attack is an attack that can make your website or application unavailable to end users. To achieve this, attackers use a variety of techniques that consume network or other resources, disrupting access for legitimate end users.

To protect your system from SoS attack, you can do the following:

1. Use an Amazon CloudFront service for distributing both static and dynamic content.
2. Use an Application Load Balancer with Auto Scaling groups for your EC2 instances then restrict direct Internet traffic to your Amazon RDS database by deploying to a private subnet.
3. Setup alerts in Amazon CloudWatch to look for high Network In and CPU utilization metrics.

Services that are available within AWS Regions, like Elastic Load Balancing and Amazon Elastic Compute Cloud (EC2), allow you to build Distributed Denial of Service resiliency and scale to handle unexpected volumes of traffic within a given region. Services that are available in AWS edge locations, like Amazon CloudFront, AWS WAF, Amazon Route53, and Amazon API Gateway, allow you to take advantage of a global network of edge locations that can provide your application with greater fault tolerance and increased scale for managing larger volumes of traffic.

In addition, you can also use AWS Shield and AWS WAF to fortify your cloud network. AWS Shield is a managed DDoS protection service that is available in two tiers: Standard and Advanced. AWS Shield Standard applies always-on detection and inline mitigation techniques, such as deterministic packet filtering and priority-based traffic shaping, to minimize application downtime and latency.

AWS WAF is a web application firewall that helps protect web applications from common web exploits that could affect application availability, compromise security, or consume excessive resources. You can use AWS WAF to define customizable web security rules that control which traffic accesses your web applications. If you use AWS Shield Advanced, you can use AWS WAF at no extra cost for those protected resources and can engage the DRT to create WAF rules.

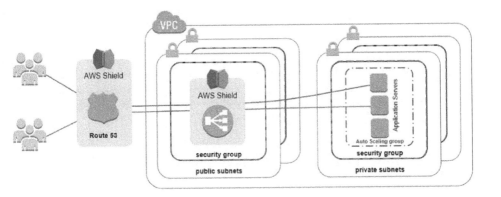

Option A is correct because using Dedicated EC2 instances are just an instance billing option. Although it may ensure that each instance has the maximum performance possible, that by itself is not enough to mitigate a DDoS attack.

Option B is correct as adding multiple elastic network interfaces (ENIs) to each EC2 instance to increase the network bandwidth is mainly done for performance improvement, and not for DDoS attack mitigation.

Options C, D and E are incorrect because they are valid mitigation techniques that can be used to prevent DDoS.

References:

https://aws.amazon.com/answers/networking/aws-ddos-attack-mitigation/

https://d0.awsstatic.com/whitepapers/DDoS_White_Paper_June2015.pdf

Best practices on DDoS Attack Mitigation:

https://youtu.be/HnoZS5jj7pk

QUESTION 32:

You are working for a tech company that uses a lot of EBS volumes in their EC2 instances. An incident occurred that requires you to delete the EBS volumes and then re-create them again. What step should you do before you delete the EBS volumes?

A. Create a copy of the EBS volume using the CopyEBSVolume command.

B. Store a snapshot of the volume. **(Correct)**

C. Download the content to an EC2 instance.

D. Back up the data into a physical disk.

EXPLANATION

You can back up the data on your Amazon EBS volumes to Amazon S3 by taking point-in-time snapshots. Snapshots are incremental backups, which means that only the blocks on the device that have changed after your most recent snapshot are saved.

When you no longer need an Amazon EBS volume, you can delete it. After deletion, its data is gone and the volume can't be attached to any instance. However, before deletion, you can store a snapshot of the volume, which you can use to re-create the volume later.

Option A is incorrect as there is no such thing as CopyEBSVolume command.

Options C and D are wrong as these actions take a lot of time. The best and easiest way is to create a snapshot.

Reference:
http://docs.aws.amazon.com/AWSEC2/latest/UserGuide/ebs-deleting-volume.html

QUESTION 33:

One of your clients is leveraging on Amazon S3 in the ap-southeast-1 region to store their training videos for their employee onboarding process. The client is storing the videos using the Standard Storage class.

Where are your client's training videos replicated?

A. A single facility in ap-southeast-1 and a single facility in eu-central-1

B. A single facility in ap-southeast-1 and a single facility in us-east-1

C. Multiple facilities in ap-southeast-1 **(Correct)**

D. A single facility in ap-southeast-1

EXPLANATION

Amazon S3 runs on the world's largest global cloud infrastructure and was built from the ground up to deliver a customer promise of 99.999999999% durability. Data is automatically distributed across a minimum of three physical facilities that are geographically separated within an AWS Region, and Amazon S3 can also automatically replicate data to any other AWS Region.

Since the Question did not say that the Cross-region replication (CRR) is enabled, then the correct answer is Option C. Amazon S3 replicates the data to multiple facilities in the same region where it is located, which is ap-southeast-1

Reference:
https://aws.amazon.com/s3/

QUESTION 34:

Your company has recently deployed a new web application which uses a serverless-based architecture in AWS. Your manager instructed you to implement CloudWatch metrics to monitor your systems more effectively. You know that Lambda automatically monitors functions on your behalf and reports metrics through Amazon CloudWatch.

In this scenario, what types of data do these metrics monitor? (Choose 2)

A. ReservedConcurrentExecutions

B. Invocations **(Correct)**

C. Errors **(Correct)**

D. IteratorSize

E. Dead Letter Queue

EXPLANATION

AWS Lambda automatically monitors functions on your behalf, reporting metrics through Amazon CloudWatch. These metrics include total invocation requests, latency, and error rates. The throttles, Dead Letter Queues errors and Iterator age for stream-based invocations are also monitored.

You can monitor metrics for Lambda and view logs by using the Lambda console, the CloudWatch console, the AWS CLI, or the CloudWatch API.

Option A is incorrect because CloudWatch does not monitor Lambda's reserved concurrent executions. You can view it through the Lambda console or via CLI manually.

Options D and E are incorrect because these two are not Lambda metrics.

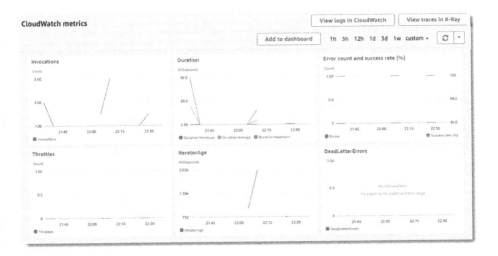

References:
https://docs.aws.amazon.com/lambda/latest/dg/monitoring-functions-access-metrics.html

https://docs.aws.amazon.com/lambda/latest/dg/monitoring-functions-metrics.html

QUESTION 35:

A company is hosting EC2 instances that are on non-production environment and processing non-priority batch loads, which can be interrupted at any time.

What is the best instance purchasing option which can be applied to your EC2 instances in this case?

A. Reserved Instances

B. On-Demand Instances

C. Spot Instances **(Correct)**

D. Scheduled Reserved Instances

EXPLANATION

Amazon EC2 Spot instances are spare compute capacity in the AWS cloud available to you at steep discounts compared to On-Demand prices. It can be interrupted by AWS EC2 with two minutes of notification when the EC2 needs the capacity back.

To use Spot Instances, you create a Spot Instance request that includes the number of instances, the instance type, the Availability Zone, and the maximum price that you are willing to pay per instance hour. If your maximum price exceeds the current Spot price, Amazon EC2 fulfills your request immediately if capacity is available. Otherwise, Amazon EC2 waits until your request can be fulfilled or until you cancel the request.

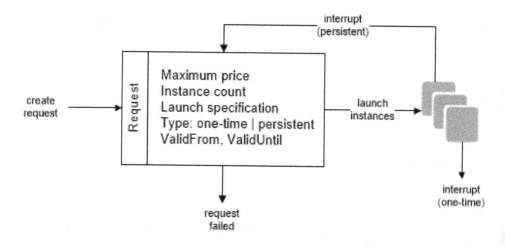

References:

http://docs.aws.amazon.com/AWSEC2/latest/UserGuide/using-spot-instances.html

https://aws.amazon.com/ec2/spot/

QUESTION 36:

You are working as a Solutions Architect for a leading airline company where you are building a decoupled application in AWS using EC2, Auto Scaling group, S3 and SQS. You designed the architecture in such a way that the EC2 instances will consume the message from the SQS queue and will automatically scale up or down based on the number of messages in the queue.

In this scenario, which of the following statements is false about SQS?

A. Standard queues provide at-least-once delivery, which means that each message is delivered at least once.

B. Standard queues preserve the order of messages. **(Correct)**

C. Amazon SQS can help you build a distributed application with decoupled components.

D. FIFO queues provide exactly-once processing.

EXPLANATION

All of the answers are correct except for Option B. Only FIFO queues can preserve the order of messages and not standard queues.

Reference:
https://aws.amazon.com/sqs/faqs/

QUESTION 37:

The media company that you are working for has a video transcoding application running on Amazon EC2. Each EC2 instance polls a queue to find out which video should be transcoded, and then runs a transcoding process. If this process is interrupted, the video will be transcoded by another instance based on the queuing system. This application has a large backlog of videos which need to be transcoded. Your manager would like to reduce this backlog by adding more EC2 instances, however, these instances are only needed until the backlog is reduced.

In this scenario, which type of Amazon EC2 instance is the most cost-effective type to use without sacrificing performance?

A. Reserved instances

B. Spot instances **(Correct)**

C. Dedicated instances

D. On-demand instances

EXPLANATION

You require an instance that will be used not as a primary server but as a spare compute resource to augment the transcoding process of your application. These instances should also be terminated once the backlog has been significantly reduced. In addition, the scenario mentions that if the current process is interrupted, the video can be transcoded by another instance based on the queuing system. This means that the application can gracefully handle an unexpected termination of an EC2 instance, like in the event of a Spot instance termination when the Spot price is greater than your set maximum price. Hence, an Amazon EC2 Spot instance is the best and cost-effective option for this scenario.

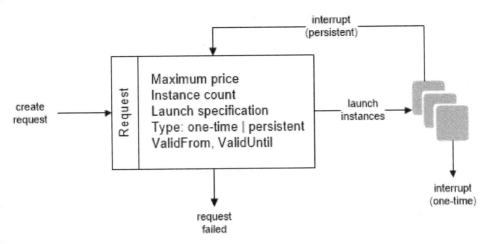

Amazon EC2 Spot instances are spare compute capacity in the AWS cloud available to you at steep discounts compared to On-Demand prices. EC2 Spot enables you to optimize your costs on the AWS cloud and scale your application's throughput up to 10X for the same budget. By simply selecting Spot when launching EC2 instances, you can save up-to 90% on On-Demand prices. The only difference between On-Demand instances and Spot Instances is that Spot instances can be interrupted by EC2 with two minutes of notification when the EC2 needs the capacity back.

You can specify whether Amazon EC2 should hibernate, stop, or terminate Spot Instances when they are interrupted. You can choose the interruption behavior that meets your needs.

Take note that there is no "bid price" anymore for Spot EC2 instances since March 2018. You simply have to set your maximum price instead.

Options A and C are incorrect as Reserved and Dedicated instances do not act as spare compute capacity.

Option D is a valid option but a Spot instance is much cheaper than On-Demand.

References:

https://docs.aws.amazon.com/AWSEC2/latest/UserGuide/spot-interruptions.html

http://docs.aws.amazon.com/AWSEC2/latest/UserGuide/how-spot-instances-work.html

https://aws.amazon.com/blogs/compute/new-amazon-ec2-spot-pricing

QUESTION 38:

You currently have an Augment Reality (AR) mobile game which has a serverless backend. It is using a DynamoDB table which was launched using the AWS CLI to store all the user data and information gathered from the players and a Lambda function to pull the data from DynamoDB. The game is being used by millions of users each day to read and store data.

How would you design the application to improve its overall performance and make it more scalable while keeping the costs low? (Choose 2)

A. Enable DynamoDB Accelerator (DAX) and ensure that the Auto Scaling is enabled and increase the maximum provisioned read and write capacity. **(Correct)**

B. Configure CloudFront with DynamoDB as the origin; cache frequently accessed data on client device using ElastiCache.

C. Use AWS SSO and Cognito to authenticate users and have them directly access DynamoDB using single-sign on. Manually set the provisioned read and write capacity to a higher RCU and WCU.

D. Use API Gateway in conjunction with Lambda and turn on the caching on frequently accessed data and enable DynamoDB global replication. **(Correct)**

E. Since Auto Scaling is enabled by default, the provisioned read and write capacity will adjust automatically. Also enable

DynamoDB Accelerator (DAX) to improve the performance from milliseconds to microseconds.

EXPLANATION

Amazon DynamoDB Accelerator (DAX) is a fully managed, highly available, in-memory cache for DynamoDB that delivers up to a 10x performance improvement – from milliseconds to microseconds – even at millions of requests per second. DAX does all the heavy lifting required to add in-memory acceleration to your DynamoDB tables, without requiring developers to manage cache invalidation, data population, or cluster management.

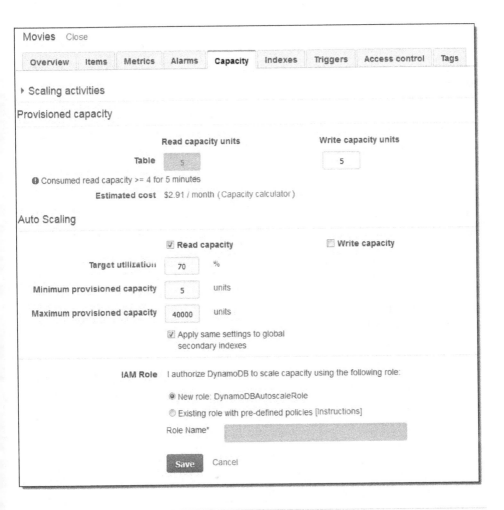

Amazon API Gateway lets you create an API that acts as a "front door" for applications to access data, business logic, or functionality from your back-end services, such as code running on AWS Lambda. Amazon API Gateway handles all of the tasks involved in accepting and processing up to hundreds of thousands of concurrent API calls, including traffic management, authorization and access control, monitoring, and API version management. Amazon API Gateway has no minimum fees or startup costs.

AWS Lambda scales your functions automatically on your behalf. Every time an event notification is received for your function, AWS Lambda quickly locates free capacity within its compute fleet and runs your code. Since your code is stateless, AWS Lambda can start as many copies of your function as needed without lengthy deployment and configuration delays.

Option B is incorrect because although CloudFront delivers content faster to your users using edge locations, you still cannot integrate DynamoDB table with CloudFront as these two are incompatible. In addition, DataSync is a data transfer service that automates moving data between on-premises storage and Amazon S3 or Amazon EFS. You should not be caching large amounts of data on a client's mobile, but rather on your side.

Option C is incorrect because AWS Single Sign-On (SSO) is a cloud SSO service that just makes it easy to centrally manage SSO access to multiple AWS accounts and business applications. This will not be of much help on the scalability and performance of the application. It is costly to manually set the provisioned read and write capacity to a higher RCU and WCU because this capacity will run round the clock and will still be the same even if the incoming traffic is stable and there is no need to scale.

Option E is incorrect because, by default, Auto Scaling is not enabled in a DynamoDB table which is created using the AWS CLI.

References:

https://aws.amazon.com/lambda/faqs/

https://aws.amazon.com/api-gateway/faqs/

https://aws.amazon.com/dynamodb/dax/

QUESTION 39:

An online job site is using NGINX for its application servers hosted in EC2 instances and MongoDB Atlas for its database-tier. MongoDB Atlas is a fully automated third-party cloud service which is not provided by AWS, but supports VPC peering to connect to your VPC.

Which of the following items are invalid VPC peering configurations? (Choose 2)

A. Two VPCs peered to a specific CIDR block in one VPC
B. Transitive Peering **(Correct)**
C. Edge to Edge routing via a gateway **(Correct)**
D. One to one relationship between two Virtual Private Cloud networks
E. One VPC Peered with two VPCs using longest prefix match

EXPLANATION

Options B and C are invalid VPC Peering configurations, while the other options are valid ones.

The following VPC peering connection configurations are not supported.

1. Overlapping CIDR Blocks
2. Transitive Peering
3. Edge to Edge Routing Through a Gateway or Private Connection

Overlapping CIDR Blocks

You cannot create a VPC peering connection between VPCs with matching or overlapping IPv4 CIDR blocks.

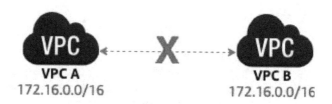

If the VPCs have multiple IPv4 CIDR blocks, you cannot create a VPC peering connection if any of the CIDR blocks overlap (regardless of whether you intend to use the VPC peering connection for communication between the non-overlapping CIDR blocks only).

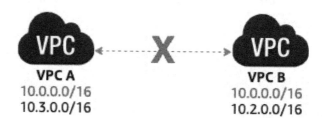

This limitation also applies to VPCs that have non-overlapping IPv6 CIDR blocks. Even if you intend to use the VPC peering connection for IPv6 communication only, you cannot create a VPC peering connection if the VPCs have matching or overlapping IPv4 CIDR blocks. Communication over IPv6 is not supported for an inter-region VPC peering connection.

Transitive Peering

You have a VPC peering connection between VPC A and VPC B (pcx-aaaabbbb), and between VPC A and VPC C (pcx-aaaacccc). There is no VPC peering connection between VPC B and VPC C. You cannot route packets directly from VPC B to VPC C through VPC A.

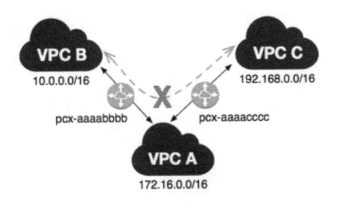

Edge to Edge Routing Through a Gateway or Private Connection

If either VPC in a peering relationship has one of the following connections, you cannot extend the peering relationship to that connection:

1. A VPN connection or an AWS Direct Connect connection to a corporate network
2. An internet connection through an internet gateway
3. An internet connection in a private subnet through a NAT device
4. A VPC endpoint to an AWS service; for example, an endpoint to Amazon S3.
5. (IPv6) A ClassicLink connection. You can enable IPv4 communication between a linked EC2-Classic instance and instances in a VPC on the other side of a VPC peering connection. However, IPv6 is not supported in EC2-Classic, so you cannot extend this connection for IPv6 communication.

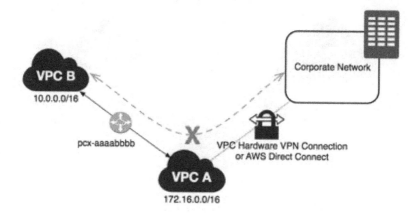

For example, if VPC A and VPC B are peered, and VPC A has any of these connections, then instances in VPC B cannot use the connection to access resources on the other side of the connection. Similarly, resources on the other side of a connection cannot use the connection to access VPC B.

References:

http://docs.aws.amazon.com/AmazonVPC/latest/PeeringGuide/invalid-peering-configurations.html

https://docs.aws.amazon.com/vpc/latest/peering/peering-configurations-partial-access.html

Here is a quick introduction to VPC Peering:

https://youtu.be/i1A1eH8vLtk

QUESTION 40:

You are a new Solutions Architect in your company. Upon checking the existing Inbound Rules of your Network ACL, you saw this configuration:

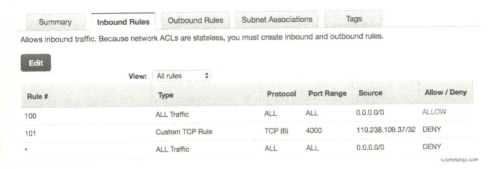

If a computer with an IP address of 110.238.109.37 sends a request to your VPC, what will happen?

A. Initially, it will be allowed and then after a while, the connection will be denied.

B. Initially, it will be denied and then after a while, the connection will be allowed.

C. It will be allowed. **(Correct)**

D. It will be denied.

EXPLANATION

Rules are evaluated starting with the lowest numbered rule. As soon as a rule matches traffic, it's applied immediately regardless of any higher-numbered rule that may contradict it.

We have 3 rules here:

1. Rule 100 permits all traffic from any source.
2. Rule 101 denies all traffic coming from 110.238.109.37
3. The Default Rule (*) denies all traffic from any source.

The Rule 100 will first be evaluated. If there is a match, then it will allow the request. Otherwise, it will then go to Rule 101 to repeat the same process until it goes to the default rule. In this case, when there is a request from 110.238.109.37, it will go through Rule 100 first. As Rule 100 says it will permit all traffic from any source, it will allow this request and will not further evaluate Rule 101 (which denies 110.238.109.37) nor the default rule.

Reference:
http://docs.aws.amazon.com/AmazonVPC/latest/UserGuide/VPC_ACLs.html

QUESTION 41:

Your company has an e-commerce application that saves the transaction logs to an S3 bucket. You are instructed by the CTO to configure the application to keep the transaction logs for one month for troubleshooting purposes, and then afterwards, purge the logs. What should you do to accomplish this requirement?

A. Add a new bucket policy on the Amazon S3 bucket.

B. Configure the lifecycle configuration rules on the Amazon S3 bucket to purge the transaction logs after a month **(Correct)**

C. Create a new IAM policy for the Amazon S3 bucket that automatically deletes the logs after a month

D. Enable CORS on the Amazon S3 bucket which will enable the automatic monthly deletion of data

EXPLANATION

In this scenario, the best way to accomplish the requirement is to simply configure the lifecycle configuration rules on the Amazon S3 bucket to purge the transaction logs after a month.

Lifecycle configuration enables you to specify the lifecycle management of objects in a bucket. The configuration is a set of one or more rules, where each rule defines an action for Amazon S3 to apply to a group of objects. These actions can be classified as follows:

- **Transition actions** – In which you define when objects transition to another storage class. For example, you may choose to transition objects to the STANDARD_IA (IA, for infrequent access) storage class 30 days after creation, or archive objects to the GLACIER storage class one year after creation.

- **Expiration actions** – In which you specify when the objects expire. Then Amazon S3 deletes the expired objects on your behalf.

Option A is incorrect as adding a new policy does not provide a solution to any of your needs in this scenario. You add a bucket policy to a bucket to grant other AWS accounts or IAM users access permissions for the bucket and the objects in it.

Option C is incorrect because IAM policies are primarily used to specify what actions are allowed or denied on your S3 buckets. You cannot configure an IAM policy to automatically purge logs for you in any way.

Option D is incorrect. CORS allows client web applications that are loaded in one domain to interact with resources in a different domain.

Reference:

https://docs.aws.amazon.com/AmazonS3/latest/dev/object-lifecycle-mgmt.html

QUESTION 42:

A company is using a custom shell script to automate the deployment and management of their EC2 instances. The script is using various AWS CLI commands such as revoke-security-group-ingress, revoke-security-group-egress, run-scheduled-instances and many others.

In the shell script, what does the revoke-security-group-ingress command do?

A. Removes one or more security groups from a rule.

B. Removes one or more security groups from an Amazon EC2 instance.

C. Removes one or more ingress rules from a security group. **(Correct)**

D. Removes one or more egress rules from a security group.

EXPLANATION

The revoke-security-group-ingress command removes one or more ingress rules from a security group.

Each rule consists of the protocol and the CIDR range or source security group. For the TCP and UDP protocols, you must also specify the destination port or range of ports. For the ICMP protocol, you must also specify the ICMP type and code. If the security group rule has a description, you do not have to specify the description to revoke the rule.

Rule changes are propagated to instances within the security group as quickly as possible. However, a small delay might occur. This example removes TCP port 22 access for the 203.0.113.0/24 address range from the security group named MySecurityGroup. If the command succeeds, no output is returned.

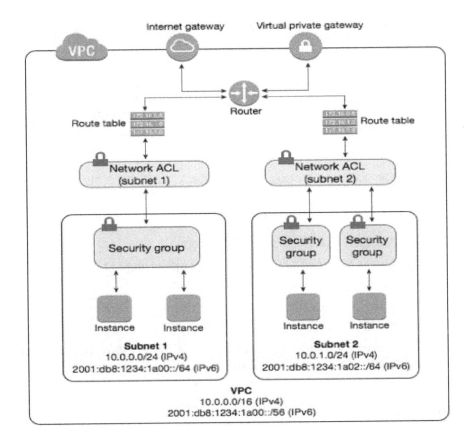

Command.

aws ec2 revoke-security-group-ingress --group-name MySecurityGroup --protocol tcp --port 22 --cidr 203.0.113.0/24

References:

https://docs.aws.amazon.com/cli/latest/reference/ec2/revoke-security-group-ingress.html

https://docs.aws.amazon.com/vpc/latest/userguide/VPC_SecurityGroups.html

QUESTION 43:

You are unable to connect to your new EC2 instance via SSH from your home computer, which you have recently deployed. However, you were able to successfully access other existing instances in your VPC without any issues.

Which of the following should you check and possibly correct to restore connectivity?

A. Use Amazon Data Lifecycle Manager.

B. Configure the Network Access Control List of your VPC to permit ingress traffic over port 22 from your IP.

C. Configure the Security Group of the EC2 instance to permit ingress traffic over port 3389 from your IP.

D. Configure the Security Group of the EC2 instance to permit ingress traffic over port 22 from your IP. **(Correct)**

EXPLANATION

When connecting to your EC2 instance via SSH, you need to ensure that port 22 is allowed on the security group of your EC2 instance.

A security group acts as a virtual firewall that controls the traffic for one or more instances. When you launch an instance, you associate one or more security groups with the instance. You add rules to each security group that allow traffic to or from its associated instances. You can modify the rules for a security group at any time; the new rules are automatically applied to all instances that are associated with the security group.

Option A is incorrect because Amazon Data Lifecycle Manager is primarily used to manage the lifecycle of your AWS resources and not to allow certain traffic to go through.

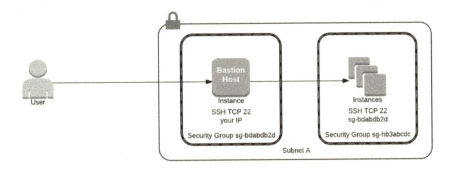

Option B is incorrect because configuring the Network Access Control List (Network ACL) is not necessary in this scenario as it was specified that you were able to connect to other EC2 instances. In addition, Network ACL is much suitable to control the traffic that goes in and out of your entire VPC and not just on one EC2 instance.

Option C is incorrect because this is relevant to RDP and not SSH.

Reference:
http://docs.aws.amazon.com/AWSEC2/latest/UserGuide/using-network-security.html

QUESTION 44:

A leading media company has an application hosted in an EBS-backed EC2 instance which uses Simple Workflow Service (SWF) to handle its sequential background jobs. The application works well in production and your manager asked you to also implement the same solution to other areas of their business.

In which other scenarios can you use both Simple Workflow Service (SWF) and Amazon EC2 as a solution? (Choose 2)

A. For a distributed session management for your mobile application.

B. Managing a multi-step and multi-decision checkout process of an e-commerce mobile app. **(Correct)**

C. Orchestrating the execution of distributed business processes **(Correct)**

D. For applications that require a message queue.

E. For web applications that require content delivery networks.

EXPLANATION

You can use a combination of EC2 and SWF for the following scenarios:

1. Managing a multi-step and multi-decision checkout process of an e-commerce mobile app.
2. Orchestrating the execution of distributed business processes

Amazon Simple Workflow Service (SWF) is a web service that makes it easy to coordinate work across distributed application components. Amazon SWF enables applications for a range of use cases, including media processing, web application back-ends, business process workflows, and analytics pipelines, to be designed as a coordination of tasks. Tasks represent invocations of various processing steps in an application which can be performed by executable code, web service calls, human actions, and scripts.

Option A is incorrect as Elasticache is the best option for distributed session management.
Option D is incorrect as SQS is the best service to use as a message queue.
Option E is incorrect as CloudFront is the best option for applications that require a global content delivery network.

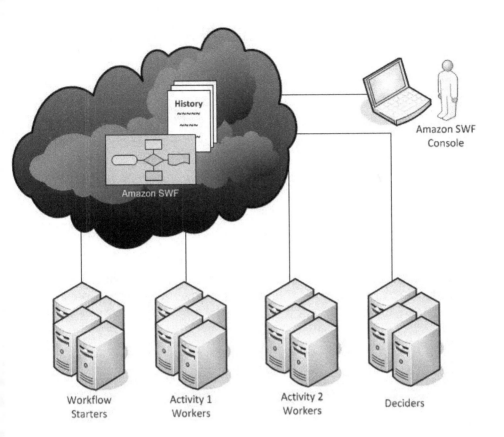

Amazon SWF Console

Amazon SWF

History

Workflow
Starters

Activity 1
Workers

Activity 2
Workers

Deciders

References:

https://aws.amazon.com/swf/

https://aws.amazon.com/ec2/

QUESTION 45:

You are a new Solutions Architect in a large insurance firm. To maintain compliance with HIPPA laws, all data being backed up or stored on Amazon S3 needs to be encrypted at rest. In this scenario, what is the best method of encryption for your data, assuming S3 is being used for storing financial-related data? (Choose 2)

A. Enable SSE on an S3 bucket to make use of AES-256 encryption **(Correct)**

B. Store the data in encrypted EBS snapshots

C. Encrypt the data locally using your own encryption keys, then copy the data to Amazon S3 over HTTPS endpoints **(Correct)**

D. Store the data on EBS volumes with encryption enabled instead of using Amazon S3

E. Use AWS Shield to protect your data at rest

EXPLANATION

Data protection refers to protecting data while in-transit (as it travels to and from Amazon S3) and at rest (while it is stored on disks in Amazon S3 data centers). You can protect data in transit by using SSL or by using client-side encryption. You have the following options for protecting data at rest in Amazon S3.

Use Server-Side Encryption – You request Amazon S3 to encrypt your object before saving it on disks in its data centers and decrypt it when you download the objects.

Use Client-Side Encryption – You can encrypt data client-side and upload the encrypted data to Amazon S3. In this case, you manage the encryption process, the encryption keys, and related tools.

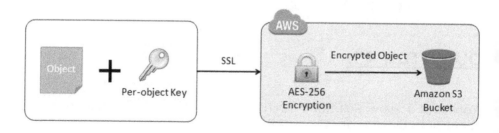

Hence, Options A and C are the correct answers:

Enable SSE on an S3 bucket to make use of AES-256 encryption

Encrypt the data locally using your own encryption keys, then copy the data to Amazon S3 over HTTPS endpoints. This refers to using a Server-Side Encryption with Customer-Provided Keys (SSE-C).

Options B and D are incorrect because all these options are for protecting your data in your EBS volumes. Note that an S3 bucket does not use EBS volumes to store your data.

Option E is incorrect because AWS Shield is mainly used to protect your entire VPC against DDoS attacks.

References:

https://docs.aws.amazon.com/AmazonS3/latest/dev/serv-side-encryption.html

https://docs.aws.amazon.com/AmazonS3/latest/dev/UsingClientSideEncryption.html

QUESTION 46:

A tech company is currently using Auto Scaling for their web application. A new AMI now needs to be used for launching a fleet of EC2 instances.

Which of the following changes needs to be done?

A. Do nothing. You can start directly launching EC2 instances in the Auto Scaling group with the same launch configuration.
B. Create a new launch configuration. **(Correct)**
C. Create a new target group.
D. Create a new target group and launch configuration.

EXPLANATION

For this scenario, you have to create a new launch configuration. Remember that you can't modify a launch configuration after you've created it.

A launch configuration is a template that an Auto Scaling group uses to launch EC2 instances. When you create a launch configuration, you specify information for the instances such as the ID of the Amazon Machine Image (AMI), the instance type, a key pair, one or more security groups, and a block device mapping. If you've launched an EC2 instance before, you specified the same information in order to launch the instance.

You can specify your launch configuration with multiple Auto Scaling groups. However, you can only specify one launch configuration for an Auto Scaling group at a time, and you can't modify a launch configuration after you've created it. Therefore, if you want to change the launch configuration for an Auto Scaling group, you must create a launch configuration and then update your Auto Scaling group with the new launch configuration.

Option A is incorrect because what you are trying to achieve is change the AMI being used by your fleet of EC2 instances. Therefore, you need to change the launch configuration to update what your instances are using.

Options C and D are incorrect because you only want to change the AMI being used by your instances, and not the instances themselves. Therefore, you should be updating your launch configuration, not the target group.

Reference:
http://docs.aws.amazon.com/autoscaling/latest/userguide/LaunchConfiguration.html

QUESTION 47:

You are working as a Cloud Engineer for a top aerospace engineering firm. One of your tasks is to set up a document storage system using

S3 for all of the engineering files. In Amazon S3, which of the following statements are true? (Choose 2)

A. The total volume of data and number of objects you can store are unlimited. **(Correct)**

B. The largest object that can be uploaded in a single PUT is 5 TB.

C. S3 is an object storage service that provides file system access semantics (such as strong consistency and file locking), and concurrently-accessible storage.

D. You can only store ZIP or TAR files in S3.

E. The largest object that can be uploaded in a single PUT is 5 GB. **(Correct)**

EXPLANATION

The correct answers are:
The total volume of data and number of objects you can store are unlimited.
The largest object that can be uploaded in a single PUT is 5 GB.

Option B is incorrect as the largest object that can be uploaded in a single PUT is 5 GB and not 5 TB. Remember that the upload limit depends on whether you upload an object using a single PUT operation or via Multipart Upload. The largest object that can be uploaded in a single PUT is 5 GB. Please take note the phrase "... in a single PUT". If you are using the multipart upload API, then the limit is 5 TB.

Option C is incorrect because although S3 is indeed an object storage service, it does not provide file system access semantics. EFS provides this feature but not S3.

Option D is incorrect as you can store virtually any kind of data in any format in S3.

References:

https://aws.amazon.com/s3/faqs/

https://docs.aws.amazon.com/AmazonS3/latest/dev/UploadingObjects.html

QUESTION 48:

You are setting up the cloud architecture for an international money transfer service to be deployed in AWS which will have thousands of users around the globe. The service should be available 24/7 to avoid any business disruption and should be resilient enough to handle the outage of an entire AWS region. To meet this requirement, you have deployed your AWS resources to multiple AWS Regions. You need to use Route 53 and configure it to set all of your resources to be available all the time as much as possible. When a resource becomes unavailable, your Route 53 should detect that it's unhealthy and stop including it when responding to queries.

Which of the following is the most fault tolerant routing configuration that you should use in this scenario?

A. Configure an Active-Active Failover with Weighted routing policy. **(Correct)**

B. Configure an Active-Passive Failover with Weighted Records.

C. Configure an Active-Active Failover with One Primary and One Secondary Resource.

D. Configure an Active-Passive Failover with Multiple Primary and Secondary Resources.

EXPLANATION

You can use Route 53 health checking to configure active-active and active-passive failover configurations. You configure active-active failover using any routing policy (or combination of routing policies) other than failover, and you configure active-passive failover using the failover routing policy.

Active-Active Failover

Use this failover configuration when you want all of your resources to be available the majority of the time. When a resource becomes unavailable, Route 53 can detect that it's unhealthy and stop including it when responding to queries.

In active-active failover, all the records that have the same name, the same type (such as A or AAAA), and the same routing policy (such as weighted or latency) are active unless Route 53 considers them unhealthy. Route 53 can respond to a DNS query using any healthy record.

Active-Passive Failover

Use an active-passive failover configuration when you want a primary resource or group of resources to be available the majority of the time and you want a secondary resource or group of resources to be on standby in case all the primary resources become unavailable. When responding to queries, Route 53 includes only the healthy primary resources. If all the primary resources are unhealthy, Route 53 begins to include only the healthy secondary resources in response to DNS queries.

Options B and D are incorrect because an Active-Passive Failover is mainly used when you want a primary resource or group of resources to be available most of the time and you want a secondary resource or group of resources to be on standby in case all the primary resources become unavailable. In this scenario, all of your resources should be available all the time as much as possible which is why you have to use an Active-Active Failover instead.

Option C is incorrect because you cannot set up an Active-Active Failover with One Primary and One Secondary Resource. Remember that an Active-Active Failover uses all available resources all the time without a primary nor a secondary resource.

References:

https://docs.aws.amazon.com/Route53/latest/DeveloperGuide/dns-failover-types.html

https://docs.aws.amazon.com/Route53/latest/DeveloperGuide/routing-policy.html

https://docs.aws.amazon.com/Route53/latest/DeveloperGuide/dns-failover-configuring.html

QUESTION 49:

You are working as a Solutions Architect for a global game development company. They have a web application currently running on twenty EC2 instances as part of an Auto Scaling group. All twenty instances have been running at a maximum of 100% CPU Utilization for the past 40 minutes however, the Auto Scaling group has not added any additional EC2 instances to the group.

What could be the root cause of this issue? (Choose 2)

A. You already have 20 on-demand instances running in your entire VPC. **(Correct)**

B. The maximum size of your Auto Scaling group is set to twenty. **(Correct)**

C. The scale down policy of your Auto Scaling group is too high.

D. The scale up policy of your Auto Scaling group, which is based on the average CPU Utilization metric, is not yet reached.

E. You are using burstable instances which have the ability to sustain high CPU performance of more than 40 minutes, which in effect, suspends your scale-up policy.

EXPLANATION

You are limited to running up to a total of 20 On-Demand instances across the instance family, purchasing 20 Reserved Instances, and requesting Spot Instances per your dynamic Spot limit per region.

If the maximum size of your Auto Scaling group has already been reached, then it would not create any new EC2 instance.

Hence, the correct answers are Options A and B:

- You already have 20 on-demand instances running in your entire VPC.

- The maximum size of your Auto Scaling group is set to twenty.

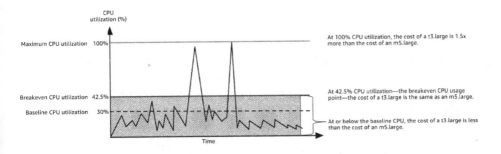

Option C is incorrect because the scenario depicts that the number of running instances is limited to 20 when you scale up, therefore, the scale down policy has nothing to do with this.

Option D is incorrect because your thresholds should have been reached since all instances are showing 100% utilization. What is preventing you from scaling is the maximum size you set for the auto scaling group.

Option E is incorrect because a burstable instance, which runs at higher CPU utilization for a prolonged period, does not affect the scale-up policy of the Auto Scaling group. Burstable instances provide additional compute capacity and cost-benefit for your EC2 instances hence, this is not a possible culprit in this scenario.

References:

https://aws.amazon.com/ec2/faqs/

https://docs.aws.amazon.com/autoscaling/ec2/userguide/as-scaling-target-tracking.html

QUESTION 50:

A new online banking platform has been re-designed to have a microservices architecture in which complex applications are decomposed into smaller, independent services. The new platform is using Docker considering that application containers are optimal for running small, decoupled services.

Which service can you use to migrate this new platform to AWS?

A. EKS

B. EFS

C. ECS **(Correct)**

D. EBS

EXPLANATION

Amazon Elastic Container Service (Amazon ECS) is a highly scalable, fast, container management service that makes it easy to run, stop, and manage Docker containers on a cluster. You can host your cluster on a serverless infrastructure that is managed by Amazon ECS by launching your services or tasks using the Fargate launch type. For more control, you can host your tasks on a cluster of Amazon Elastic Compute Cloud (Amazon EC2) instances that you manage by using the EC2 launch type.

Option A is incorrect because Amazon EKS runs the Kubernetes management infrastructure and not Docker.

Option B is incorrect because Amazon EFS is a file system for Linux-based workloads for use with AWS Cloud services and on-premises resources.

Option D is incorrect because Amazon EBS is primarily used to provide persistent block storage volumes for use with Amazon EC2 instances in the AWS Cloud.

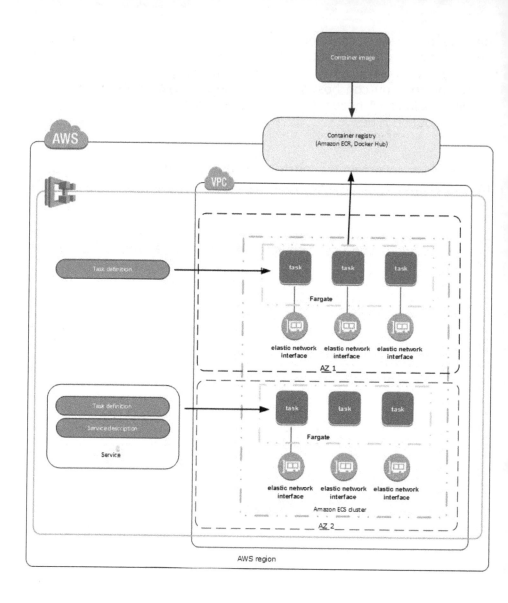

Reference:

https://docs.aws.amazon.com/AmazonECS/latest/developerguide/Welcome.html

QUESTION 51:

You are working for a large telecommunications company where you need to run analytics against all combined log files from your Application Load Balancer as part of the regulatory requirements.

Which AWS services can be used together to collect logs and then easily perform log analysis?

A. Amazon DynamoDB for storing and EC2 for analyzing the logs.

B. Amazon EC2 with EBS volumes for storing and analyzing the log files.

C. Amazon S3 for storing the ELB log files and an EC2 instance for analyzing the log files using a custom-built application.

D. Amazon S3 for storing ELB log files and Amazon EMR for analyzing the log files. **(Correct)**

EXPLANATION

In this scenario, it is best to use a combination of Amazon S3 and Amazon EMR: Amazon S3 for storing ELB log files and Amazon EMR for analyzing the log files. Access logging in the ELB is stored in Amazon S3 which means that Options C and 4 are both valid answers. However, log analysis can be automatically provided by Amazon EMR, which is more economical than building a custom-built log analysis application and hosting it in EC2. Hence, Option D is the best answer between the two.

Access logging is an optional feature of Elastic Load Balancing that is disabled by default. After you enable access logging for your load balancer, Elastic Load Balancing captures the logs and stores them in the Amazon S3 bucket that you specify as compressed files. You can disable access logging at any time.

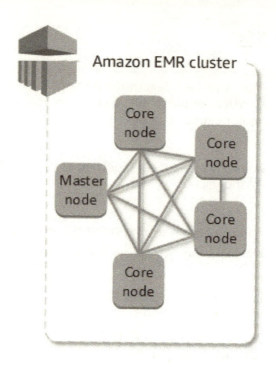

Amazon EMR cluster

Core node

Core node

Master node

Core node

Core node

Core node

Amazon EMR provides a managed Hadoop framework that makes it easy, fast, and cost-effective to process vast amounts of data across dynamically scalable Amazon EC2 instances. It securely and reliably handles a broad set of big data use cases, including log analysis, web indexing, data transformations (ETL), machine learning, financial analysis, scientific simulation, and bioinformatics. You can also run other popular distributed frameworks such as Apache Spark, HBase, Presto, and Flink in Amazon EMR, and interact with data in other AWS data stores such as Amazon S3 and Amazon DynamoDB.

Option A is incorrect because DynamoDB is a noSQL database solution of AWS. It would be inefficient to store logs in DynamoDB while using EC2 to analyze them.

Option B is incorrect because using EC2 with EBS would be costly, and EBS might not provide the most durable storage for your logs, unlike S3.

Option C is incorrect because using EC2 to analyze logs would be inefficient and expensive since you will have to program the analyzer yourself.

References:

https://aws.amazon.com/emr/

https://docs.aws.amazon.com/elasticloadbalancing/latest/application/load-balancer-access-logs.html

QUESTION 52:

Your company is in a hurry of deploying their new web application written in NodeJS to AWS. As the Solutions Architect of the company, you were assigned to do the deployment without worrying about the underlying infrastructure that runs the application. Which service will you use to easily deploy and manage your new web application in AWS?

A. AWS Elastic Beanstalk **(Correct)**

B. AWS CloudFront

C. AWS CloudFormation

D. AWS CodeCommit

EXPLANATION

With Elastic Beanstalk, you can quickly deploy and manage applications in the AWS Cloud without worrying about the infrastructure that runs those applications. AWS Elastic Beanstalk reduces management complexity without restricting choice or control. You simply upload your application, and Elastic Beanstalk automatically handles the details of capacity provisioning, load balancing, scaling, and application health monitoring.

Option B is incorrect because AWS CloudFront is a fast content delivery network (CDN) service that securely delivers data, videos, applications, and APIs to customers globally with low latency and high transfer speeds. It does not provide any deployment capability for your custom applications unlike Elastic Beanstalk.

Option C is incorrect because although the CloudFormation service provides deployment capabilities, you will still have to design a custom template that contains the required AWS resources for your application needs. Hence, this will require more time to complete instead of just directly using Elastic Beanstalk.

Option D is incorrect because although you can upload your NodeJS code in AWS CloudCommit, this service is just a fully-managed source control service that hosts secure Git-based repositiories and hence, it does not provide a way to deploy or manage your applications in AWS.

Reference:
https://docs.aws.amazon.com/elasticbeanstalk/latest/dg/Welcome.html

QUESTION 53:

Your web application is relying entirely on slower disk-based databases, causing it to perform slowly. To improve its performance, you integrated an in-memory data store to your web application using ElastiCache. How does Amazon ElastiCache improve database performance?

A. It securely delivers data to customers globally with low latency and high transfer speeds.

B. It provides an in-memory cache that delivers up to 10x performance improvement from milliseconds to microseconds or even at millions of requests per second.

C. By caching database query results. **(Correct)**

D. It reduces the load on your database by routing read queries from your applications to the Read Replica.

EXPLANATION

ElastiCache improves the performance of your database through caching query results.

The primary purpose of an in-memory key-value store is to provide ultra-fast (submillisecond latency) and inexpensive access to copies of data. Most data stores have areas of data that are frequently accessed but seldom updated. Additionally, querying a database is always slower and more expensive than locating a key in a key-value pair cache. Some database queries are especially expensive to perform, for example, queries that involve joins across multiple tables or queries with intensive calculations.

By caching such query results, you pay the price of the query once and then are able to quickly retrieve the data multiple times without having to re-execute the query.

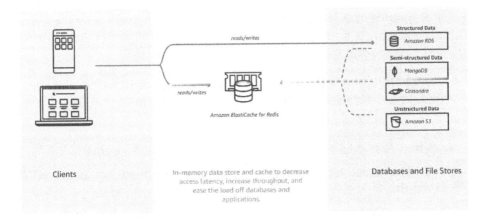

Clients   In-memory data store and cache to decrease   Databases and File Stores
               access latency, increase throughput, and
               ease the load off databases and
               applications.

Option A is incorrect because this option describes what CloudFront does and not ElastiCache.

Option B is incorrect because this option describes what Amazon DynamoDB Accelerator (DAX) does and not ElastiCache. Amazon DynamoDB Accelerator (DAX) is a fully managed, highly available, in-memory cache for DynamoDB.

Option D is incorrect because this option describes what an RDS Read Replica does and not ElastiCache. Amazon RDS Read Replicas enable you to create one or more read-only copies of your database instance within the same AWS Region or in a different AWS Region.

References:

https://aws.amazon.com/elasticache/

https://docs.aws.amazon.com/AmazonElastiCache/latest/red-ug/elasticache-use-cases.html

QUESTION 54:

In your VPC, you have a Classic Load Balancer distributing traffic to 2 running EC2 instances in ap-southeast-1a AZ and 8 EC2 instances in ap-southeast-1b AZ. However, you noticed that half of your incoming traffic goes to ap-southeast-1a AZ which over-utilize its 2 instances but underutilize the other 8 instances in the other AZ.

What could be the most likely cause of this problem?

A. The Classic Load Balancer listener is not set to port 80.
B. The security group of the EC2 instances does not allow HTTP traffic.
C. Cross-Zone Load Balancing is disabled. (Correct)
D. The Classic Load Balancer listener is not set to port 22.

EXPLANATION

Cross-zone load balancing reduces the need to maintain equivalent numbers of instances in each enabled Availability Zone, and improves your application's ability to handle the loss of one or more instances.

When you create a Classic Load Balancer, the default for cross-zone load balancing depends on how you create the load balancer. With the API or CLI, cross-zone load balancing is disabled by default. With the AWS Management Console, the option to enable cross-zone load balancing is selected by default. After you create a Classic Load Balancer, you can enable or disable cross-zone load balancing at any time.

The following diagrams demonstrate the effect of cross-zone load balancing. There are two enabled Availability Zones, with 2 targets in Availability Zone A and 8 targets in Availability Zone B. Clients send requests, and Amazon Route 53 responds to each request with the IP address of one of the load balancer nodes. This distributes traffic such that each load balancer node receives 50% of the traffic from the clients. Each load balancer node distributes its share of the traffic across the registered targets in its scope.

If cross-zone load balancing is enabled, each of the 10 targets receives 10% of the traffic. This is because each load balancer node can route its 50% of the client traffic to all 10 targets.

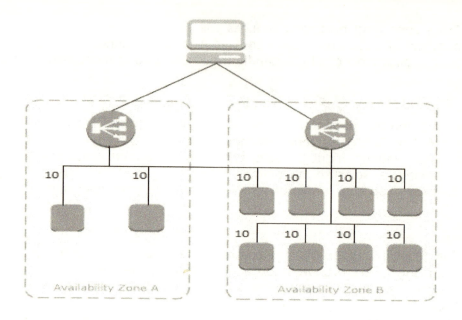

If cross-zone load balancing is disabled, each of the 2 targets in Availability Zone A receives 25% of the traffic and each of the 8 targets in Availability Zone B receives 6.25% of the traffic. This is because each load balancer node can route its 50% of the client traffic only to targets in its Availability Zone.

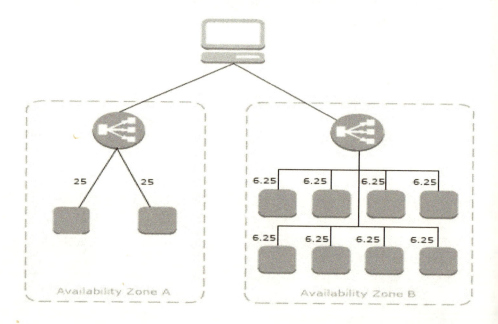

References:

https://docs.aws.amazon.com/elasticloadbalancing/latest/userguide/how-elastic-load-balancing-works.html#cross-zone-load-balancing

http://docs.aws.amazon.com/elasticloadbalancing/latest/classic/enable-disable-crosszone-lb.htm

QUESTION 55:

You are trying to convince a team to use Amazon RDS Read Replica for your multi-tier web application. What are two benefits of using read replicas? (Choose 2)

A. It provides elasticity to your Amazon RDS database. **(Correct)**

B. Allows both read and write operations on the read replica to complement the primary database.

C. Improves performance of the primary database by taking workload from it. **(Correct)**

D. Automatic failover in the case of Availability Zone service failures.

E. It enhances the read performance of your primary database.

EXPLANATION

Amazon RDS Read Replicas provide enhanced performance and durability for database (DB) instances. This feature makes it easy to elastically scale out beyond the capacity constraints of a single DB instance for read-heavy database workloads.

You can create one or more replicas of a given source DB Instance and serve high-volume application read traffic from multiple copies of your data, thereby increasing aggregate read throughput. Read replicas can also be promoted when needed to become standalone DB instances. Read replicas are available in Amazon RDS for MySQL, MariaDB, Oracle and PostgreSQL, as well as Amazon Aurora.

Option B is incorrect as Read Replicas are primarily used to offload read operations from the primary database instance.

Option D is incorrect as this is a benefit of Multi-AZ and not of a Read Replica.

Option E is incorrect because Read Replicas do not do anything to upgrade or increase the read throughput on the primary DB instance per se, but it provides a way for your application to fetch data from replicas. In this way, it improves the overall performance of your entire database-tier (and not just the primary DB instance).

Reference:
https://aws.amazon.com/rds/details/read-replicas/

 Additional tutorial - How do I make my RDS MySQL read replica writable?

https://youtu.be/j5da6d2TIPc

QUESTION 56:

You have a VPC that has a CIDR block of 10.31.0.0/27 which is connected to your on-premises data center. There was a requirement to create a Lambda function that will process massive amounts of cryptocurrency transactions every minute and then store the results to EFS. After you set up the serverless architecture and connected Lambda function to your VPC, you noticed that there is an increase in invocation errors with EC2 error types such as EC2ThrottledException on certain times of the day.

Which of the following are the possible causes of this issue? (Choose 2)

A. You only specified one subnet in your Lambda function configuration. That single subnet runs out of available IP addresses and there is no other subnet or Availability Zone which can handle the peak load. **(Correct)**

B. Your VPC does not have a NAT gateway.

C. Your VPC does not have sufficient subnet ENIs or subnet IPs. **(Correct)**

D. The associated security group of your function does not allow outbound connections.

E. The attached IAM execution role of your function does not have the necessary permissions to access the resources of your VPC.

EXPLANATION

You can configure a function to connect to a virtual private cloud (VPC) in your account. Use Amazon Virtual Private Cloud (Amazon VPC) to create a private network for resources such as databases, cache instances, or internal services. Connect your function to the VPC to access private resources during execution.

AWS Lambda runs your function code securely within a VPC by default. However, to enable your Lambda function to access resources inside your private VPC, you must provide additional VPC-specific configuration information that includes VPC subnet IDs and security group IDs. AWS Lambda uses this information to set up elastic network interfaces (ENIs) that enable your function to connect securely to other resources within your private VPC.

Lambda functions cannot connect directly to a VPC with dedicated instance tenancy. To connect to resources in a dedicated VPC, peer it to a second VPC with default tenancy.

https://youtu.be/JcRKdEP94jM

Your Lambda function automatically scales based on the number of events it processes. If your Lambda function accesses a VPC, you must make sure that your VPC has sufficient ENI capacity to support the scale requirements of your Lambda function. It is also recommended that you specify at least one subnet in each Availability Zone in your Lambda function configuration.

By specifying subnets in each of the Availability Zones, your Lambda function can run in another Availability Zone if one goes down or runs out of IP addresses. If your VPC does not have sufficient ENIs or subnet IPs, your Lambda function will not scale as requests increase, and you will see an increase in invocation errors with EC2 error types like EC2ThrottledException. For asynchronous invocation, if you see an increase in errors without corresponding CloudWatch Logs, invoke the Lambda function synchronously in the console to get the error responses. Hence, the correct answers for this scenario are Options A and C.

Option B is incorrect because an issue in the NAT Gateway is unlikely to cause a request throttling issue or produce an EC2ThrottledException error in Lambda. Take note that the scenario says that the issue is happening only on certain times of the day, which means that the issue is only intermittent and the function works at other times. We can also conclude that an availability issue is not an issue since the application is already using a highly available NAT Gateway and not just a NAT instance.

Option D is incorrect because if the associated security group does not allow outbound connections then the Lambda function will not work at all in the first place. Remember that the scenario says that the issue only happens intermittently. In addition, Internet traffic restrictions do not usually produce EC2ThrottledException errors.

Option E is incorrect because just as what is explained in Options B and D above, the issue is intermittent and thus, the IAM execution role of the function does have the necessary permissions to access the resources of the VPC since it works at those specific times. In case that the issue is indeed caused by a permission problem, then an EC2AccessDeniedException error would most likely be returned and not an EC2ThrottledException error.

References:

https://docs.aws.amazon.com/lambda/latest/dg/vpc.html

https://aws.amazon.com/premiumsupport/knowledge-center/internet-access-lambda-function/

QUESTION 57:

You are a Solutions Architect working for an aerospace engineering company which recently adopted a hybrid cloud infrastructure with AWS. One of your tasks is to launch a VPC with both public and private subnets for their EC2 instances as well as their database instances respectively.

Which of the following statements are true regarding Amazon VPC subnets? (Choose 2)

A. EC2 instances in a private subnet can communicate with the Internet only if they have an Elastic IP.

B. Each subnet maps to a single Availability Zone. **(Correct)**

C. The allowed block size in VPC is between a /16 netmask (65,536 IP addresses) and /27 netmask (16 IP addresses).

D. Every subnet that you create is automatically associated with the main route table for the VPC.**(Correct)**

E. Each subnet spans to 2 Availability Zones.

EXPLANATION

A VPC spans all the Availability Zones in the region. After creating a VPC, you can add one or more subnets in each Availability Zone. When you create a subnet, you specify the CIDR block for the subnet, which is a subset of the VPC CIDR block. Each subnet must reside entirely within one Availability Zone and cannot span zones. Availability Zones are distinct locations that are engineered to be isolated from failures in other Availability Zones. By launching instances in separate Availability Zones, you can protect your applications from the failure of a single location.

Below are the important points you have to remember about subnets:

-Each subnet maps to a single Availability Zone.
-Every subnet that you create is automatically associated with the main route table for the VPC.
-If a subnet's traffic is routed to an Internet gateway, the subnet is known as a public subnet.

Option A is incorrect because EC2 instances in a private subnet can communicate with the Internet not just by having an Elastic IP, but also with a public IP address.

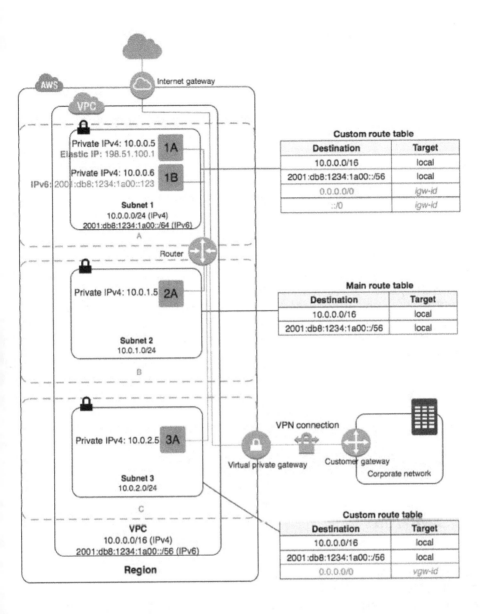

Custom route table

Destination	Target
10.0.0.0/16	local
2001:db8:1234:1a00::/56	local
0.0.0.0/0	igw-id
::/0	igw-id

Main route table

Destination	Target
10.0.0.0/16	local
2001:db8:1234:1a00::/56	local

Custom route table

Destination	Target
10.0.0.0/16	local
2001:db8:1234:1a00::/56	local
0.0.0.0/0	vgw-id

Option C is incorrect because the allowed block size in VPC is between a /16 netmask (65,536 IP addresses) and /28 netmask (16 IP addresses) and not /27 netmask. For you to easily remember this, /27 netmask is equivalent to exactly 27 IP addresses but keep in mind that the limit is until /28 netmask.

Option E is incorrect because each subnet must reside entirely within one Availability Zone and cannot span zones.

Reference:
https://docs.aws.amazon.com/AmazonVPC/latest/UserGuide/VPC_Sub nets.html

QUESTION 58:

You are working as a Solutions Architect for a tech company where you are instructed to build a web architecture using On-Demand EC2 instances and a database in AWS. However, due to budget constraints, the company instructed you to choose a database service in which they no longer need to worry about database management tasks such as hardware or software provisioning, setup, configuration, scaling and backups. Which database service in AWS is best to use in this scenario?

A. AWS RDS

B. DynamoDB **(Correct)**

C. Amazon ElastiCache

D. Redshift

EXPLANATION

Basically, a database service in which you no longer need to worry about database management tasks such as hardware or software provisioning, setup and configuration is called a fully managed database. This means that AWS fully manages all of the database management tasks and the underlying host server. The main differentiator here is the keyword "scaling" in the question. In RDS, you still have to manually scale up your resources and create Read Replicas to improve scalability while in DynamoDB, this is automatically done.

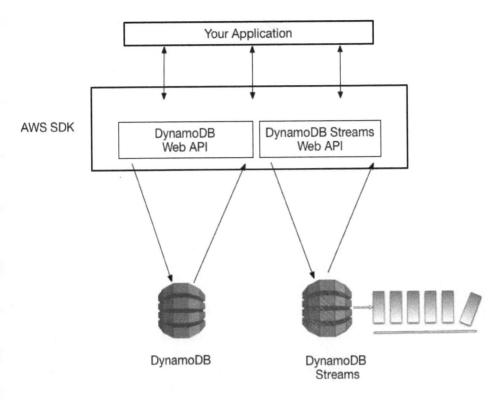

DynamoDB is the best option to use in this scenario. It is a fully managed non-relational database service – you simply create a database table, set your target utilization for Auto Scaling, and let the service handle the rest. You no longer need to worry about database management tasks such as hardware or software provisioning, setup and configuration, software patching, operating a reliable, distributed database cluster, or partitioning data over multiple instances as you scale. DynamoDB also lets you backup and restore all your tables for data archival, helping you meet your corporate and governmental regulatory requirements

Option A is incorrect because AWS RDS is just a "managed" service and not "fully managed". This means that you still have to handle the backups and other administrative tasks such as when the automated OS patching will take place.

Option C is incorrect because although ElastiCache is fully managed, it is not a database service but an In-Memory Data Store.

Option D is incorrect because although Redshift is fully managed, it is not a database service but a Data Warehouse.

References:

https://aws.amazon.com/dynamodb/

https://aws.amazon.com/products/databases/

QUESTION 59:

You are a Solutions Architect for a major TV network. They have a web application running on eight Amazon EC2 instances, consuming about 55% of resources on each instance. You are using Auto Scaling to make sure that eight instances are running at all times. The number of requests that this application processes are consistent and do not experience spikes. Your manager instructed you to ensure high availability of this web application at all times to avoid any loss of revenue. You want the load to be distributed evenly between all instances. You also want to use the same Amazon Machine Image (AMI) for all EC2 instances.

How will you be able to achieve this?

A. Deploy eight EC2 instances with Auto Scaling in one Availability Zone behind an Amazon Elastic Load Balancer.

B. Deploy four EC2 instances with Auto Scaling in one region and four in another region behind an Amazon Elastic Load Balancer.

C. Deploy four EC2 instances with Auto Scaling in one Availability Zone and four in another availability zone in the same region behind an Amazon Elastic Load Balancer. **(Correct)**

D. Deploy two EC2 instances with Auto Scaling in four regions behind an Amazon Elastic Load Balancer.

EXPLANATION

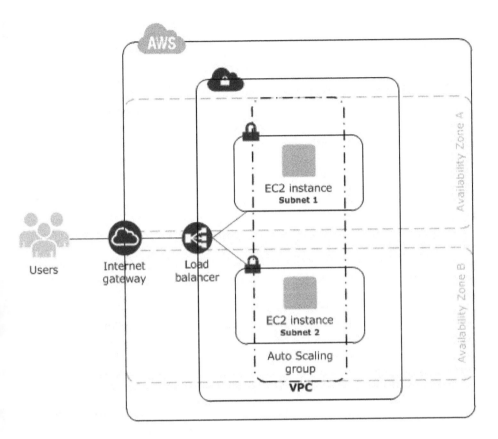

The best option to take is to deploy four EC2 instances in one Availability Zone and four in another availability zone in the same region behind an Amazon Elastic Load Balancer. In this way, if one availability zone goes down, there is still another available zone that can accommodate traffic.

Take note that Auto Scaling will launch additional EC2 instances to the remaining Availability Zone/s in the event of an Availability Zone outage in the region. Hence, Option C is correct.

Option A is incorrect because this architecture is not highly available. If that Availability Zone goes down then your web application will be unreachable.

Options B and D are incorrect because the ELB is designed to only run in one region and not across multiple regions.

References:

https://aws.amazon.com/elasticloadbalancing/

https://docs.aws.amazon.com/AWSEC2/latest/UserGuide/ec2-increase-availability.html

QUESTION 60:

Your IT Manager instructed you to set up a bastion host in the cheapest, most secure way, and that you should be the only person that can access it via SSH.

Which of the following steps would satisfy your IT Manager's request?

A. Set up a small EC2 instance and a security group which only allows access on port 22 via your IP address **(Correct)**

B. Set up a large EC2 instance and a security group which only allows access on port 22 via your IP address

C. Set up a large EC2 instance and a security group which only allows access on port 22

D. Set up a small EC2 instance and a security group which only allows access on port 22

EXPLANATION

A bastion host is a server whose purpose is to provide access to a private network from an external network, such as the Internet. Because of its exposure to potential attack, a bastion host must minimize the chances of penetration.

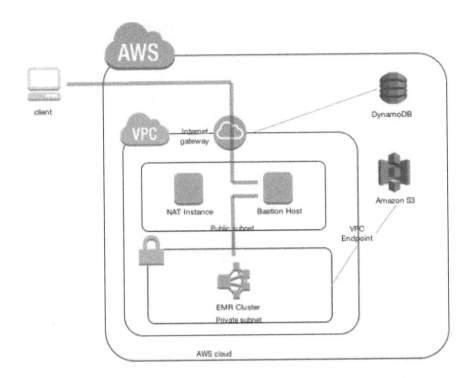

To create a bastion host, you can create a new EC2 instance which should only have a security group from a particular IP address for maximum security. Since the cost is also considered in the question, you should choose a small instance for your host. By default, t2.micro instance is used by AWS but you can change these settings during deployment.

Option B is incorrect because you don't need to provision a large EC2 instance to run a single bastion host. At the same time, you are looking for the cheapest solution possible.

Options C and D are incorrect because you did not set your specific IP address to the security group rules, which possibly means that you publicly allow traffic from all sources in your security group. This is wrong as you should only be the one to have access to the bastion host.

References:

https://docs.aws.amazon.com/quickstart/latest/linux-bastion/architecture.html

https://aws.amazon.com/blogs/security/how-to-record-ssh-sessions-established-through-a-bastion-host/

QUESTION 61:

In Amazon EC2, you can manage your instances from the moment you launch them up to their termination. You can flexibly control your computing costs by changing the EC2 instance state. Which of the following statements is true regarding EC2 billing? (Choose 2)

A. You will be billed when your On-Demand instance is in pending state.

B. You will be billed when your Spot instance is preparing to stop with a stopping state.

C. You will be billed when your On-Demand instance is preparing to hibernate with a stopping state. **(Correct)**

D. You will be billed when your Reserved instance is in terminated state. **(Correct)**

E. You will not be billed for any instance usage while an instance is not in the running state.

EXPLANATION

By working with Amazon EC2 to manage your instances from the moment you launch them through their termination, you ensure that your customers have the best possible experience with the applications or sites that you host on your instances. The following illustration represents the transitions between instance states. Notice that you can't stop and start an instance store-backed instance:

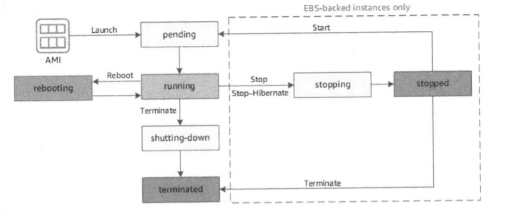

Below are the valid EC2 lifecycle instance states:

pending - The instance is preparing to enter the running state. An instance enters the pending state when it launches for the first time, or when it is restarted after being in the stopped state.

running - The instance is running and ready for use.

stopping - The instance is preparing to be stopped. Take note that you will not billed if it is preparing to stop however, you will still be billed if it is just preparing to hibernate.

stopped - The instance is shut down and cannot be used. The instance can be restarted at any time.

shutting-down - The instance is preparing to be terminated.

terminated - The instance has been permanently deleted and cannot be restarted. Take note that Reserved Instances that applied to terminated instances are still billed until the end of their term according to their payment option.

Option A is incorrect because you will not be billed if your instance is in pending state.

Option B is incorrect because you will not be billed if your instance is preparing to stop with a stopping state.

Option C is correct because when the instance state is stopping, you will not billed if it is preparing to stop however, you will still be billed if it is just preparing to hibernate.

Option D is correct because Reserved Instances that applied to terminated instances are still billed until the end of their term according to their payment option. I actually raised a pull-request to Amazon team about the billing conditions for Reserved Instances, which has been approved and reflected on your official AWS Documentation: https://github.com/awsdocs/amazon-ec2-user-guide/pull/45

Option E is incorrect because the statement is not entirely true. You can still be billed if your instance is preparing to hibernate with a stopping state.

References:

https://github.com/awsdocs/amazon-ec2-user-guide/pull/45

http://docs.aws.amazon.com/AWSEC2/latest/UserGuide/ec2-instance-lifecycle.html

QUESTION 62:

You are a new Solutions Architect in your department and you have created 7 CloudFormation templates. Each template has been defined for a specific purpose.

What determines the cost of using these new CloudFormation templates?

A. $2.50 per template per month

B. The length of time it takes to build the architecture with CloudFormation

C. It depends on the region where you will deploy.

D. CloudFormation templates are free but you are charged for the underlying resources it builds. **(Correct)**

EXPLANATION

There is no additional charge for AWS CloudFormation. You pay for AWS resources (such as Amazon EC2 instances, Elastic Load Balancing load balancers, etc.) created using AWS CloudFormation in the same manner as if you created them manually. You only pay for what you use, as you use it; there are no minimum fees and no required upfront commitments.

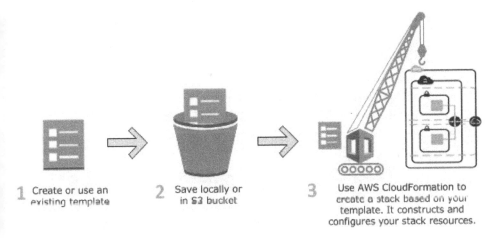

1 Create or use an existing template

2 Save locally or in S3 bucket

3 Use AWS CloudFormation to create a stack based on your template. It constructs and configures your stack resources.

Option A is incorrect. There is no cost for creating CloudFormation templates. Costs are calculated from the AWS resources that are provisioned from that CloudFormation template.

Option B is incorrect. There is no cost for the time it takes to execute CloudFormation templates. Costs are calculated from the AWS resources that are provisioned from that CloudFormation template.

Option C is incorrect. Costs per region are not calculated based on the CloudFormation template, but rather on the regions where resources are provisioned during the building of the environment using the CloudFormation template.

Reference:
https://aws.amazon.com/cloudformation/pricing/

QUESTION 63:

You are working for a large financial firm and you are instructed to set up a Linux bastion host. It will allow access to the Amazon EC2 instances running in their VPC. For security purposes, only the clients connecting from the corporate external public IP address 175.45.116.100 should have SSH access to the host.

Which is the best option that can meet the customer's requirement?

A. Security Group Inbound Rule: Protocol – TCP. Port Range – 22, Source 175.45.116.100/32 **(Correct)**

B. Security Group Inbound Rule: Protocol – UDP, Port Range – 22, Source 175.45.116.100/32

C. Network ACL Inbound Rule: Protocol – UDP, Port Range – 22, Source 175.45.116.100/32

D. Network ACL Inbound Rule: Protocol – TCP, Port Range-22, Source 175.45.116.100/0

EXPLANATION

A bastion host is a special purpose computer on a network specifically designed and configured to withstand attacks. The computer generally hosts a single application, for example a proxy server, and all other services are removed or limited to reduce the threat to the computer.

When setting up a bastion host in AWS, you should only allow the individual IP of the client and not the entire network. Therefore, in the Source, the proper CIDR notation should be used. The /32 denotes one IP address and the /0 refers to the entire network.

Option B is incorrect since the SSH protocol uses TCP and port 22, and not UDP.

Option C is incorrect since the SSH protocol uses TCP and port 22, and not UDP. Aside from that, network ACLs act as a firewall for your whole VPC subnet, while security groups operate on an instance level. Since you are securing an EC2 instance, you should be using security groups.

Option D is incorrect as it allowed the entire network instead of a single IP to gain access to the host.

Reference:
http://docs.aws.amazon.com/AWSEC2/latest/UserGuide/ec2-instance-metadata.html

QUESTION 64:

Your customer has clients all across the globe that access product files stored in several S3 buckets, which are behind each of their own CloudFront web distributions. They currently want to deliver their content to a specific client, and they need to make sure that only that client can access the data. Currently, all of their clients can access their S3 buckets directly using an S3 URL or through their CloudFront distribution.

Which of the following are possible solutions that you could implement to meet the above requirements?

A. Use CloudFront Signed Cookies to ensure that only their client can access the files.

B. Use CloudFront signed URLs to ensure that only their client can access the files.

C. Use S3 pre-signed URLs to ensure that only their client can access the files. Remove permission to use Amazon S3 URLs to read the files for anyone else. **(Correct)**

D. Create an origin access identity (OAI) and give it permission to read the files in the bucket.

EXPLANATION

Many companies that distribute content over the Internet want to restrict access to documents, business data, media streams, or content that is intended for selected users, for example, users who have paid a fee. To securely serve this private content by using CloudFront, you can do the following:

-Require that your users access your private content by using special CloudFront signed URLs or signed cookies.

-Require that your users access your Amazon S3 content by using CloudFront URLs, not Amazon S3 URLs. Requiring CloudFront URLs isn't necessary, but it is recommended to prevent users from bypassing the restrictions that you specify in signed URLs or signed cookies.

All objects and buckets by default are private. The presigned URLs are useful if you want your user/customer to be able to upload a specific object to your bucket, but you don't require them to have AWS security credentials or permissions. You can generate a presigned URL programmatically using the AWS SDK for Java or the AWS SDK for .NET. If you are using Microsoft Visual Studio, you can also use AWS Explorer to generate a presigned object URL without writing any code. Anyone who receives a valid presigned URL can then programmatically upload an object.

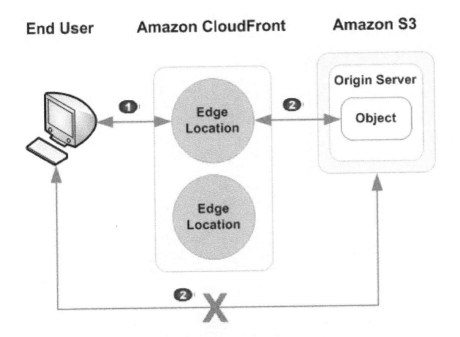

End User   **Amazon CloudFront**   **Amazon S3**

Option C is correct because using a presigned URL to your S3 bucket will prevent other users from accessing your private data which is intended only for a certain client.

Option A is incorrect because the signed cookies feature is primarily used if you want to provide access to multiple restricted files, for example, all of the files for a video in HLS format or all of the files in the subscribers' area of website. In addition, this solution is not complete since the users can bypass the restrictions by simply using the direct S3 URLs.

Option B is incorrect because although this solution is valid, the users can still bypass the restrictions in CloudFront by simply connecting to the direct S3 URLs.

Option D is incorrect because an Origin Access Identity (OAI) will require your client to access the files only by using the CloudFront URL and not through a direct S3 URL. This can be a possible solution if it mentions the use of Signed URL or Signed Cookies.

References:

https://docs.aws.amazon.com/AmazonCloudFront/latest/DeveloperGui
de/PrivateContent.html

https://docs.aws.amazon.com/AmazonS3/latest/dev/PresignedUrlUplo
adObject.html

QUESTION 65:

A travel company has a suite of web applications hosted in an Auto Scaling group of On-Demand EC2 instances behind an Application Load Balancer that handles traffic from various web domains such as i-love-manila.com, i-love-boracay.com, i-love-cebu.com and many others. To improve security and lessen the overall cost, you are instructed to secure the system by allowing multiple domains to serve SSL traffic without the need to reauthenticate and reprovision your certificate everytime you add a new domain. This migration from HTTP to HTTPS will help improve their SEO and Google search ranking.

Which of the following is the most cost-effective solution to meet the above requirement?

A. Use a wildcard certificate to handle multiple sub-domains and different domains.

B. Add a Subject Alternative Name (SAN) for each additional domain to your certificate.

C. Create a new CloudFront web distribution and configure it to serve HTTPS requests using dedicated IP addresses in order to associate your alternate domain names with a dedicated IP address in each CloudFront edge location.

D. Upload all SSL certificates of the domains in the ALB using the console and bind multiple certificates to the same secure listener on your load balancer. ALB will automatically choose the optimal TLS certificate for each client using Server Name Indication (SNI). **(Correct)**

EXPLANATION

SNI Custom SSL relies on the SNI extension of the Transport Layer Security protocol, which allows multiple domains to serve SSL traffic over the same IP address by including the hostname which the viewers are trying to connect to.

You can host multiple TLS secured applications, each with its own TLS certificate, behind a single load balancer. In order to use SNI, all you need to do is bind multiple certificates to the same secure listener on your load balancer. ALB will automatically choose the optimal TLS certificate for each client. These features are provided at no additional charge.

To meet the requirements in the scenario, you can upload all SSL certificates of the domains in the ALB using the console and bind multiple certificates to the same secure listener on your load balancer. ALB will automatically choose the optimal TLS certificate for each client using Server Name Indication (SNI). Hence, Option D is correct.

Option A is incorrect because a wildcard certificate can only handle multiple sub-domains but not different domains.

Option B is incorrect because although using Subject Alternative Name (SAN) is correct, you will still have to reauthenticate and reprovision your certificate every time you add a new domain. One of the requirements in the scenario is that you should not have to reauthenticate and reprovision your certificate hence, this solution is incorrect.

Option C is incorrect because although it is valid to use dedicated IP addresses to meet this requirement, this solution is not cost-effective. Remember that if you configure CloudFront to serve HTTPS requests using dedicated IP addresses, you incur an additional monthly charge. The charge begins when you associate your SSL/TLS certificate with your CloudFront distribution. You can just simply upload the certificates to the ALB and use SNI to handle multiple domains in a cost-effective manner.

References:

https://aws.amazon.com/blogs/aws/new-application-load-balancer-sni/

https://docs.aws.amazon.com/AmazonCloudFront/latest/DeveloperGuide/cnames-https-dedicated-ip-or-sni.html#cnames-https-dedicated-ip

https://docs.aws.amazon.com/elasticloadbalancing/latest/application/create-https-listener.html

www.ingramcontent.com/pod-product-compliance
Lightning Source LLC
Chambersburg PA
CBHW031242050326
40690CB00007B/918